D1519921

Recovery from Depression

To Phyllis

Recovery from Depression

A Self-Help Strategy

Ari Kiev, M.D.

E. P. DUTTON · NEW YORK

Published in the United States by
E. P. Dutton, Inc., 2 Park Avenue, New York, N.Y. 10016

Library of Congress Cataloging in Publication Data
Kiev, Ari.
Recovery from depression.
1. Depression, Mental. I. Title
RC537.K525 1982   616.85'27   81-17529
AACR2

ISBN: 0-525-93239-9

Published simultaneously in Canada by
Clarke, Irwin & Company Limited, Toronto and
Vancouver

Designed by Nancy Etheredge

10   9   8   7   6   5   4   3   2   1

First Edition

Contents

[ix]

Introduction

Depression, the most common psychiatric disorder, is often difficult to recognize because so many
of the changes of mood, thought, and behavior
associated with it also occur normally in response
to the stresses of everyday life.

Clinically significant depression may be said
to exist when the duration and severity of symptoms begin to interfere with normal functioning
and cannot be eliminated by pep talks or diver-
sions.

The feelings and behavior that the depressed
person experiences are indeed distressing and
often difficult to understand, so much so, in fact,
that the person often blames himself or herself for
causing it. Depression, however, develops from a

complex combination of physical, biochemical, psychological, and social factors that make certain individuals susceptible under certain conditions. Though the specific biological mechanism is as yet unknown, recent breakthroughs in neurophysiology offer hope for an answer in the near future. One widely held view is that the stress from managing certain life crises—including serious physical illness, divorce, or the death of a loved one—sets in motion certain biochemical or physical changes in the brain that, in turn, produce the symptoms of depression, and which persist even after the crisis has passed, unalleviated by will power or positive thinking alone.

Rapid reduction of symptoms, the most immediate goal of treatment, can be accomplished with antidepressant and tranquilizing medicine alone or in combination with psychotherapy. Beyond this, the Life Strategy approach outlined in this book can help you achieve a more productive and satisfying life. Based on my work with many thousands of depressed people in both individual therapy and Life Strategy Workshops, the approach was designed to help each person assume responsibility for his or her own actions and to provide tools for handling distressing feelings. The Life Strategy approach was also designed to assist you to deal with a range of experiences, to master inner responses, and to learn what you have to change to avoid creating or heightening problems.

The techniques offered here can supplement more intensive therapy for those who are clinically depressed and can also be used alone by those with a mild depression arising from life problems.

Although each person's problems require individual solutions, there are underlying similarities in the feelings and difficulties experienced by depressed people. Because I felt that you, the reader, would find it most helpful, I have presented the strategies taught in my workshops in the form of answers to the most common questions people ask about depression. By putting these strategies into practice you can begin to gain greater control over your thoughts, moods, and behavior so that you can gradually change the way in which you experience the world, your method of solving the problems you encounter, and the general way your life develops as it changes.

Because many people generally live their lives in terms of what others expect instead of recognizing and meeting their own needs, I have focused on ways to increase the sense of self and have provided tools that have been successful in my practice in helping people to direct their own lives. Techniques that show you how to determine your natural strengths will help to establish personally meaningful goals related to those strengths. In addition there are proven stress reduction techniques that can free you to achieve maximum performance. The Life Strategy approach also offers concrete ways of improving the quality of your relationships and the ability to communicate your feelings more effectively.

With this small book as a guide, you should find it possible to develop a greater degree of self-reliance and the increased satisfactions that come when you begin to take charge of your own life.

If you are interested in attending one of Dr. Ari Kiev's Life Strategy workshops, please write to the Social Psychiatry Research Institute, 150 E. 69th Street, New York, NY 10021.

Recovery from Depression

1.

How to Recognize Depression and Begin to Help Yourself

1. I've been depressed before, but never for so long. Are there different types of depression? How can I tell them apart?

Depression has many meanings. It refers to a mood; a symptom; a psychological reaction characterized by a reduction in energy, loss of enthusiasm, and feelings of guilt and sadness; and a clinical syndrome of psychological changes that are secondary to very specific biological changes. This last is called a clinical depression. While each of the forms of depression is quite distinct in terms of the intensity and duration of symptoms, all are characterized by some degree of psychological discomfort.

Most of us talk about "being in a depressed

mood" or "feeling blue" from time to time. But these feelings are usually very short-lived and can be easily modified by a change of pace and scenery. The same may be said for the symptom of depression, which may occur in response to an obvious disappointment such as not getting into a school we wanted to attend or not getting the job we wanted. Other longer-lasting periods of depression occur when we are grieving over the loss of a loved one.

Clinical depressions are usually much longer lasting and debilitating than the other forms and can so consume the sufferer with despair that he or she may at times feel suicidal. This form of depression may be said to exist when there is no specific history of severe stress, such as the death of a loved one or a divorce *or* if the reaction to such a stressful experience is unusually intense, and prolonged, perhaps lasting longer than a year.

Clinical depression is also likely to exist if there has been a prior history of depression unrelated to any specific stressful events.

Abraham Lincoln, Nathaniel Hawthorne, Winston Churchill, Sigmund Freud, and astronaut Buzz Aldrin, to name only a few accomplished people, all had recurrent bouts of clinical depression. Churchill even had a name for his. He called it "my black dog." So if you're suffering from this kind of depression, you're not exactly in bad company.

All of these famous people managed to ride out their depressions, and that points to a crucial fact about the disorder: Depressions are self-limiting; none lasts forever. You may already have had a hint of this if you have had recurrent depressions. So you can take heart from the fact that whether or not you are treated medically, your depression will eventually come to an end.

2. What are the symptoms of clinical depression?

No doubt you are familiar with the daily fluctuations of mood, the ups and downs that most people have. If you are clinically depressed, these ups and downs will be much more intense, especially during the early hours of the morning—so fighting extra hard to get up and get going may be a hopeless and frustrating experience.

A long-term clinical depression, as compared with "the blues," can be a pretty awful thing, because its specific symptoms, both physical and psychological, seem to nourish the feelings of despair. You wake up too early in the morning after sleeping fitfully the night before. You lose interest in food, sex, and friends, as well as your usual activities. You have no energy. Your arms and legs feel heavy. You suffer from headaches, irritability, and suicidal thoughts. You have feelings of dread, which paralyze you when you get up, then mysteriously disappear sometime in the afternoon. You worry about everything, and because you worry, you can't concentrate, and that makes you worry more. Moreover, you can't make decisions and your future looks bleak.

You may begin to feel alienated and reluctant to assume responsibility or follow any routine. You may have trouble expressing yourself or asserting your point of view. You feel unappreciated, unloved, even worthless. External pressures, which seem overwhelming, make you angry, yet you are convinced you shouldn't feel that way and that you are strange or sick because you do. You're afraid to get angry with people you feel are pressuring you, because you might explode, go to pieces, or clobber someone. As bad as you feel, you're most afraid of losing control and doing something that will make you feel even more guilty.

To top it off, you feel trapped in a situation you cannot change, and that is making you feel helpless. You feel your depression will never end, that no one will ever understand you, and that it's useless to try to do anything about it.

3. How long does a clinical depression usually last? Can I do anything to shorten it?

The typical clinical depression usually lasts from three to six months, although some may lift after only a few weeks and others can continue for as long as a year. Unlike "the blues," which seem to respond to ordinary distractions or a change of activities, and grief reactions, which respond to support and the passage of time, clinical depressions are much more resistant and cannot be modified by willpower or positive thinking. The only way to speed up recovery from these depressions is through the use of active antidepressant medication, which will generally reduce the duration of depression in most instances to a period of six to eight weeks.

4. What about the weird feeling of standing outside myself?

That feeling, a common occurrence in depression, is called depersonalization. It's a form of anxiety

[5]

as well as what we call a defense mechanism—your mind's way of turning off your feelings of intolerable frustration by convincing you that the whole thing is out of your hands. If you don't understand how such a mechanism works, you can be very frightened by it, since it leaves you feeling that nothing is real, that your mind is separate from your body. This explains the feeling of numbness some people describe that leads them to want to cut themselves to see if they'll bleed. It is often experienced as a feeling of being afraid of "losing your mind."

5. *Is it normal to feel alienated from people when you are depressed?*

Yes. You may have difficulty in relating to others. A thick, invisible glass wall seems to divide you from everybody you know and gives you the feeling of being trapped inside your own body. Paradoxically, at the same time, everybody seems to be pushing you to do this or do that, to be this way or that way; nobody leaves you enough elbow room to do what *you* want to do. And since you're not at all sure yourself what that is, you're an easy mark for unsolicited suggestions, advice, and help.

6. How common are morbid thoughts such as of suicide?

Very common. When you are depressed, you are often preoccupied with recurring morbid thoughts, in addition to an extreme sense of guilt about your inability to act. The same images keep jamming your head, coming back over and over again, until all you want to do is get rid of them. You feel like hitting your head against the wall or jumping out of the window. Thoughts of suicide rise up. You push them down, but they keep returning. You don't want to die, but sometimes you feel as if that would be better than putting up with your own troubled mind. Horrifying as it seems to you, suicide sometimes looks like the only way to rid yourself of your intolerable tensions.

For this reason I always advise my patients to remove all weapons and certain potentially dangerous medications from the environment. Recent studies suggest that suicide attempts are often beyond the individual's control and that they often occur impulsively. Insofar as the suicidal drive is often brief, many suicides and suicide attempts can be prevented by not having the means available to those who in a moment of desperation might use them. Guns, in particular, should be removed from the home. Guns account for approximately 10,000 deaths by suicide in the United States each year. Poisons, barbiturates, and other potent medications also should be eliminated from the home. Barbiturates (sleeping medications) may so alter consciousness that the individual may be unaware of taking excessive amounts and may take a lethal overdose accidentally.

7. Are you suggesting that someone can get too angry at himself—even suicidal—about feeling depressed?

Yes. Not only do you feel bad *about* feeling bad, but the longer the cycle of depression-anger-depression goes on, the worse you feel for letting it continue, and the more intolerant of yourself you become. It doesn't help a bit to know that other people have felt, and are still feeling, the same way, because you are locked firmly into your own situation. Far from being reassured by knowing that depression is common, you feel surrounded by a wall of darkness, an impenetrable barrier, which prevents you from reaching out to other people.

You are likely to feel isolated and lonely. You

may feel your life is a "mess." You can't see any "light at the end of the tunnel," and you may not even be able to remember how the tunnel started. You feel overwhelmed and even the most routine tasks are more than you can manage. You have trouble making decisions, and no matter which ones you make, they always seem to be wrong. You're frustrated, defeated, and angry. No matter what you do, you can't seem to feel anything but down.

Since most emergencies develop out of a failure to recognize the early warning signs of impending difficulty, it is important that you be aware of any changes in symptoms. If there is an intensification of the following symptoms of depression, it is advisable to contact your doctor:

- Sleep difficulties
- Preoccupation with sad thoughts
- Preoccupation with the disposition of possessions and arrangements of unfinished business
- Poor appetite or compulsive overeating
- Loss of interest in the surroundings and in usual activities
- Loss of the ability to derive pleasure from the usual interests
- Loss of sexual desire
- Self-neglect

[9]

- Crying and tearfulness
- Lack of concentration and memory troubles
- Hopelessness; suicidal thoughts or threats
- Feelings of persecution
- Unexplainable lifting of mood, euphoria, or excitement
- Sudden calm in the midst of agitation

8. Is it a good idea to try to cover up these feelings?

These are pretty hard feelings to live with, and there is an inclination to try to bury them by pretending they don't exist, by acting just the opposite to the way you are feeling. Bad as you feel inside, you do what's expected of you with a stiff smile. Like somebody constantly on stage, you keep your true emotions hidden.

On the surface your acting will probably work. Most people don't recognize your inner turmoil, and so you'll successfully avoid a lot of questions, conflicts, and complaints. But you'll use an enormous amount of energy to do this, and that energy will be subtracted from other areas of your life. If you work hard at your disguise, you won't have time for much else, and you'll lose interest in things that used to please you.

9. Is that why I'm so tired? Still, I feel safer disguising my feelings. What harm is there in that?

Now, holding in feelings can really tie you up in knots. This is because it is very difficult to function as if you feel normal and strong when in fact you feel terrible. Feeling terrible and disguising it means that a lot of the time you're angry with *yourself* as well as with other people, because you're constantly refusing to stand up for the way you really feel. For many people, hiding bad feelings leads to resentment and guilt at not being genuine, and this in turn can intensify a depression.

10. Why do I feel as if no one cares, especially those that I know love me?

It's not uncommon in depression to feel utterly pessimistic about the chances of anyone else—a parent, husband, wife, friend, or doctor—being able to help you through your nightmare. It's as if no one has a handle on your inner torture. Most people are not very good listeners. If they are concerned about you, they are likely to feel guilty about you but won't know how to break through the wall around you. It's for this reason that they preach rather than listen. They may mean well, but their advice usually comes down to a facile admonition to snap out of it and get down to work. Which only makes you feel worse. Their puritanical, commonsense approach to your difficulties might work fine under ordinary circumstances, but when you're depressed, it's exactly the wrong approach. On top of this you may be adding to your feelings of guilt and inadequacy by trying to maintain your own high standards of performance and an image of competence when you would be better off to relinquish some responsibilities and reach out for others to help you.

11. Why do I feel so helpless?

Your usual way of solving problems—willpower, a stiff upper lip, increased efforts to overcome your feelings, or conscientious hard work—is not likely to be successful. This failure is what produces a sense of helplessness.

You may also feel guilty and inadequate because your reduced energy prevents you from pursuing your usual activities. Retarded functioning is part of the illness and not within your control. Additional pressure only serves to heighten your sense of being a burden.

Trying to overcompensate for being too rough on you, close relatives may sometimes go out of their way to do you little favors, to buy you unexpected presents, and generally to protect you by kindness from the trouble you are carrying inside. But this is no more helpful than their demands. It only makes you feel like an overgrown grade schooler, more helpless than ever before.

Your friends may not be much better. They, too, may mean well when they brush off your problems as insignificant, when they say, "Come on, forget it. Let's go to a movie." But they are really no more in touch with your true feelings of fear and resentment than your relatives. Their demands that you "look on the bright side" only reinforce your conviction that they cannot, or will not, penetrate your invisible wall.

12. What can I do to get people to understand the way I feel?

My advice is to do very little, which may put all the good intentions of those around you in perspective. It's the first thing you'll have to keep in mind if you want to get to that light at the end of the tunnel—the startlingly simple fact that you, and only you, can really say how you are feeling and what you should be doing about it. No one else can ever fully comprehend your feelings. It is important to remember this when others try to be helpful, for in their eagerness they sometimes unwittingly involve you in obligations that can actually escalate, rather than diminish, your problems. In trying to live up to their expectations of you, you can end up feeling worse than ever. In trying to keep your mind, as they advise, on the bright side, you may simply come to realize the truth of Tennyson's observation that "sorrow's crown of sorrow is remembering happier things." It may be useful to give them this book to read. If they understand more about depression, they're likely to be less demanding of you.

13. Are you suggesting that it's a good idea to "tune out"?

Yes. Against all the dictates of so-called common sense, I would suggest that you ignore the urgings of others that you get moving again, and the predictions that everything will be all right as soon as you take charge of your life. Sure, adversity can be overcome through effort—but not when your energy is down. Sure, great things can be accomplished by willpower—but not when you're depressed. The simplistic idea that you should "keep going" to overcome your depression is just not good advice; in fact, the harder you push yourself to function normally when you're depressed, the more likely you are to end up feeling worse. You're already being hard enough on yourself, after all. It's not a wise course to add to your feelings of resentment and frustration by forcing yourself to do things you just don't feel up to.

14. What are the basic causes of depression?

First of all, depressions are not due to a lack of willpower. Nor are they a result of laziness. You are not goofing off when you can't get up in the morning, and you're not faking it or looking for sympathy when you can't sleep or can't make a decision. You must understand what those around you too often forget—that no one wants to feel depressed, or to experience the distress of insomnia, energy loss, and fear. If you are experiencing these things, it does not mean you are a moral or physical coward.

As far as doctors know, depression is the result of certain physiological responses to stress, to which some people are more predisposed than others. That's all. It's not a curse or an irreversible condition or a cross you must bear forever. It's a physical and mental phenomenon that can be treated successfully with specific medicine.

15. How do antidepressant medications work?

The physiological response to stress that manifests itself in the form of clinical depression is characterized by a reduction in the levels of circulating neurotransmitters—neurohormones in the brain that relay information from one neuron to the next. Antidepressants work by increasing the levels of nerve transmitters in the central nervous system.

The medicines have none of the potential for addiction that alcohol and street drugs have, and they relieve the symptoms of depression simply and rapidly. With recent scientific breakthroughs in our knowledge about the nerve transmitters, sleep cycles, and biological or circadian rhythms, we can anticipate the development of newer and even more effective medicines in the years ahead.

If there is a family history of mood disturbances and you have experienced repeated episodes of depression and/or various degrees of euphoria (from mild elation to the more extreme and rarer forms of mania) that occur without any relationship to stressful life events, you may be a candidate for prophylactic or preventive therapy with lithium carbonate. This relatively new form of treatment with a naturally occurring salt, the amount of which can actually be measured in your blood for accurate levels, has proved effective in preventing repeated episodes of this condition and has reduced the suffering of many millions of people.

I'm not trying to persuade you to visit your doctor (who can prescribe such medicines) or even to see a psychiatrist. I simply want you to know that specific medical relief is available if your symptoms persist too long. Whether you opt for this course of action or you decide to ride through the depression on your own, you should know that it can be dealt with.

16. How long does it take for the antidepressant medication to work?

It takes several days for the antidepressant medicines to reach therapeutic levels in the bloodstream, so that immediate relief of symptoms is rarely possible. Knowing this can make waiting somewhat easier. During the initial phase of chemotherapy, before any noticeable benefit can take place, side effects such as drowsiness, constipation, and dry mouth may be experienced. These usually disappear, or become tolerable, after a short period of time. Doubts about the usefulness of the medicine should be discussed with a doctor, who is the only person qualified to prescribe medication and evaluate its results. Friends and relatives are not trained to do this and should refrain from making decisions in this matter.

Don't undermine your own confidence and faith in the treatment by discussing the doubts you and your relatives might have about it. While a second opinion can certainly help in the initial selection of physicians or clinics, once treatment has begun, discussion of it with others can only serve to confuse you. Concerned relatives should discuss these issues beforehand, only with your doctor and only after securing your permission to do so.

Depression requires professional assessment and treatment, just as physical illnesses do. Don't let others become involved in solving your problems. The hardest thing in the world for concerned relatives to do is to keep from offering friendly advice or from trying out their own form of therapy. It is best not to allow them to push or prod you to discuss your difficulties in an effort to "understand" the causes of your distress. This may only intensify your preoccupations. Discussions of this nature should be left to the doctor.

17. What else should I do when I'm depressed?

Well, if you had a broken leg, you wouldn't expect to jog two miles a day or keep going to football practice while it mended. You'd stay off your feet for a while and take it easy. If you were running a high fever, you wouldn't jump in a pool and start doing laps. You'd get in bed and rest until you were better. Essentially you should use the same kind of caution when you're depressed. Don't push yourself, but find a level of activity at which you can function comfortably.

18. What if I can't get moving at all?

If you're feeling so bad that you don't want to get out of bed to face the day, stay there. Take it easy for a while; a brief time out from your responsibilities can be beneficial, in spite of what seems like common sense. It makes more sense to treat yourself like a patient than to force yourself to perform when you can't. "While grief is fresh," said Samuel Johnson, "every attempt to divert only irritates. You must wait till it be digested, and then amusement will dissipate the remains."

19. How do I explain "taking it easy" to others?

This is difficult to do, since most people don't understand this concept. It runs counter to everything you've been told up to now by your friends and relatives, perhaps even your doctors. People close to you are especially likely to have trouble with the suggestion that you take it easy for a while, because their eagerness to see you back to normal makes it hard for them to understand your staying in bed.

I know it's difficult to resist them and to resist feeling guilty for disappointing them, but only you can decide when you're ready to get up and face the world. Remember that disguising your feelings of helplessness by mock bravado can actually intensify them, while giving in for a time to the way you feel can gradually release the pressure and make you feel less tense.

Doing this, of course, means taking your problem seriously even though those around you may not be willing to do so. People who try to comfort those who are depressed often minimize, and sometimes even ignore, what is going on under their noses. They may attribute your difficulties to the stresses of your particular life period, whether it be adolescence or midlife crisis or growing old, or explain your loss of interest in school or work as merely temporary and unimportant, even normal for your age. Yet you know that not all people going through the same experiences feel depressed, and you sense, even if you cannot put it into words, that what is troubling you is something more serious than just a passing stage or life crisis. If your loss of initiative, your inefficiency, your listlessness, and the other problems you describe are taken as normal occurrences for your age or your circumstances, your chances of overcoming them will be greatly reduced. You can overcome them, as I hope to show you, but first you must recognize them as unique, serious, and real.

A depression often develops when usual methods of coping with life's problems have failed. It can be a turning point, especially if you seek professional help, and begin to take a new and different look at yourself and your relationships with others. Frequently, more healthy and satisfying ways of living and relating to others can evolve from the changes that take place during and after a depression.

But recognizing that you have a problem is only the beginning. Next you must find a way to overcome it. I hope you will take my advice before you begin to do that, and take that short breather first. Relax and take a slow, hard look at the invisible wall around you. Then stay with me while I see if I can show you a way to surmount it.

2.

Planning a Life Strategy

1. I feel overwhelmed by a sense of inertia. How do I get back into an active life? Is inertia part of depression?

Useful as it may be for you to sit back and relax for a while, eventually you're going to need to get out of bed, confront the wall around you, and get your life moving again. I know this isn't easy. Once you've relaxed—once you've gotten used to inactivity—the natural tendency is to let it take over. The force that physicists call inertia—the force that keeps moving objects moving and stopped objects at rest—frequently proves of greater power than anybody's purpose or will.

When you're depressed, inertia has a real edge on you, because along with the guilt and resentment you often have a heightened awareness of the absurdity of life, which makes you wonder if there's any point in going on. Since no one is connecting with you, the attempt to make sense of your life can seem pointless and unreal. This feeling of rejection and emptiness, the sense of futility that is sometimes called existential despair, comes over every one of us at one time or another.

2. It's true that I feel rejected, and yet I can't quite figure out what's going on. Where do feelings of rejection originate?

Essentially feelings of rejection arise as a result of the progressively decreasing support we get from our parents, and later our friends, as we grow older. When we're infants, pretty much everything we do is applauded. As we grow, however, we're obliged to learn certain appropriate ways of doing things and to avoid others. When you were young, your parents probably very often showed you the right way to perform certain tasks, and although this was meant to help you, it also implied that the way you were doing it was wrong—and that you were wrong as well. Most of us have this experience as children, and as a result, at the root of our sense of self is some feeling about not being "okay."

Parents often take your strengths for granted and focus attention on your weaknesses so you can become stronger. This can leave you with some residue of bad feelings about yourself. Such feelings can make you feel inadequate, unloved, and unlovable. Even though we all learn to cover up such recognitions of our own fallibility, we understand they are there. As we learn to behave in socially acceptable ways, we sense that those who respond to our social side are ignoring our negative side, and as a result we never feel fully accepted, even when we reach the presumably serene years of middle life.

3. Can you explain my feeling of being so isolated?

If you feel isolated, it is probably because you fear being rejected or ridiculed for your secret "negative" side. For this reason you communicate in roundabout ways. You're probably not sure what you want to communicate, and you may even fail to comprehend what others are trying to say— what they want or need. Just as you begin to assert your identity in relation to others, you may become painfully aware of the complex connection between thought and language and begin to see how complicated communication can be.

4. Do feelings of suspicion sometimes occur in depression?

Yes. Some of your anxiety may be unrealistic. Like most of us, you may misperceive the intentions and expectations of other people, suspecting ill will or deviousness where none exists. So aware are you when you're depressed that you are a secret sinner that you may imagine everyone else must be aware of this, too.

5. What about failures? I have those too.

Very common. On top of misperceptions of difficulty you may experience actual, tangible evidence that you are a failure. Even if until now you've always been at the top of the heap, slowly but surely this situation is beginning to end. Throughout life you go through a lot of changes and may experience a number of major stresses such as illness, loss of loved ones, economic reversals, as well as real rejections and conflicts in your relationships with friends and relatives. Given the likelihood of disappointments and stress, it's not surprising that you are disconsolate and confused some of the time.

It wouldn't be surprising either if you viewed the requests and suggestions of others not as honest offers of help, but as badgering, nagging demands, especially if you are experiencing the inertia of depression. No wonder you are having trouble in knowing whose advice to follow, and even in knowing what all those outside voices want of you. Your inclination is to try to meet the expectations of others, but are you perceiving them correctly? You wonder sometimes how anyone can have your best interests at heart if they are so inclined to pressure you—and this makes you buck them just for spite.

But it's not just close friends and relatives. You probably haven't learned to say no to the demands of acquaintances or associates either—demands that often conflict with your own expectations. You're tired of having others tell you what to do, but you're not confident enough yet to be able to tell yourself. And you don't want to alienate people, because that would make the wall thicker than it already is.

You may feel that pressures are coming at you from all sides. No matter how hard you try, they just don't let up. When you think you've got one problem licked, another one rears its head.

Like a character in a Western movie, just as you've sized up the guy in front of you, you're nailed by somebody who has sneaked in the back door with a shotgun.

6. What about the anxiety I feel? What can I do to control it?

That feeling of being surrounded can be frightening, but when you think about it, you know it will pass in time or at least become less significant. Some of the distress you feel is like the pregame jitters or the stage fright most of us get just before a race or a speech. Some of this results from uncertainty and the unfamiliarity of the situation; some of it results from excessive efforts to eliminate the tension, which can actually create more of it. Once you learn how to flow with your anxiety rather than eliminate it, you will see that your distress is not going to last forever, and you will feel more comfortable and be better able to cope with your pressures. If in addition you can stop doing the things that intensify your distress (which tend to be activities chosen by others and not by "trusting your instincts"), it will pass much quicker.

In this connection I would remind you that a lot of your negative thoughts come from bottled up feelings (especially angry feelings), which you are reluctant to express except self-destructively toward yourself. Your self-destructive thoughts really reflect your suppressed desire to assert yourself, and to the extent that you can learn to acknowledge your feelings, you will become less self-destructive and more self-creative.

In fact, if you can learn to relinquish responsibility for all those who have made you feel responsible for their peace of mind and can become more self-assertive and less dependent on their approval, you will have moved a long way in this direction.

7. *Is there any value in suffering?*

I don't want to romanticize depression, because we both know it's not very glamorous or pleasant, but if it can be said to have a virtue it's that it usually leads to growth. "Out of suffering," said E. H. Chapin, "emerge the strongest souls." By going through these difficult times now, you will gain greater self-awareness and develop a firmer sense of your own identity. When you feel defeated and discouraged about the future, remember what the great American writer Henry Ward Beecher said about defeat: "It is defeat that turns bone to flint, and gristle to muscle, and makes men invincible and formed those heroic natures that are now in ascendancy in the world. Do not then be afraid of defeat—You are never so near to victory as when defeated in a good cause."

8. You seem to be suggesting I have hidden strengths rather than that I set limits on my personal expectations?

Sooner or later you have got to recognize your limits, but in doing so you will be moving in the direction of discovering your talents or hidden potential and will begin to live life as it was meant to be lived—independently, not pseudoindependently.

In his essay "Spiritual Laws," Emerson described this phenomenon: "Each man has his own vocation. The talent is the call. There is one direction in which all space is open to him. He has faculties silently inviting him thither to endless exertion. He is like a ship in a river; he runs against obstructions on every side but one; on that side all obstruction is taken away, and he sweeps serenely over a deepening channel into an infinite sea."

The earlier you can discover your own unique potential the sooner you will begin to assume responsibility for yourself.

9. How would you advise me about making decisions?

All through life we are faced with decisions, with opportunities to define our identity and take a stand on issues. Most of us at one time or another want to do this but hold back out of a fear of failure or ridicule. Even when you have felt overworked, you have been unable to ask for help. Sometimes you know what you want but can't bring yourself to request it. Consciously or unconsciously you maneuver others into sharing decisions with you because of a fear that you will be judged too aggressive if you make them for yourself. In trying to deny your true feelings, however, you generate enormous stress and in the end make poor decisions. This is why, no matter what you decide, it always seems to be wrong. If you can start to make decisions without worrying what others will think of them, you will be on the road to defining yourself rather than having others tell you who you are. And isn't that what everyone really wants to do?

I think too that you may be afraid to let yourself feel good, afraid others will reject you for taking something (happiness) that you don't believe you deserve. You may even search out situations where you can be seen suffering to avoid having to face the fact that you secretly don't want to be happy.

10. Are there specific strategies I can follow to improve my life?

You can begin to turn your life around by looking at your present situation as a turning point of your life—a moment when you can take the first steps toward leading a life in accord with your own unique desires. You may think you've come to the end of the line, but there is nothing objectively accurate about that assessment. It is a subjective judgment you can change. If you can begin to look closely at important problems in your life and try to start solving them in accordance with your own, and not others', needs then your depression will begin to lift, and you will learn to function productively in spite of the unavoidable stresses of daily life.

11. You've said several times that I should start to choose what satisfies my own needs and talents best. But how do I learn to do that? Is it too late?

It is never too late to start moving your life in the direction of your choices. I have known patients in their seventies, even eighties, who were able to modify certain aspects of their life circumstances and make their later years truly golden ones. Oliver Wendell Holmes wrote some of his best works when he was in his seventies. Goethe completed *Faust* at eighty. And Titian painted his historic masterpiece, *The Battle of Lepanto*, at age ninety-eight.

To find these talents you must be willing to try a variety of activities until you find the ones that click for you; since ultimately, satisfaction comes from making the most of your own specific talents and capabilities. Duplicating what others have done can never give you the gratification that developing your own interests can, nor can anyone tell you what is your best choice.

When you take a journey, you keep moving, trying to cover as much territory as possible. Each day you get up early in anticipation of new sights, sounds, smells, and experiences. Some days are good and some are rotten, but each one offers new opportunities, and if you keep moving, you are bound to have some good times along the way. In addition, the more you travel, the better you get at it. You learn how to handle foreign currencies without getting ripped off. You learn where to drink the water and where not to. You learn what kinds of sites turn you on and which ones you'd just as soon avoid. When I first began traveling, I always went to the recommended places, the "right" spots on the map. But as I continued, I found more and more that the places I was supposed to see just didn't interest me, so I gradually learned to revise my itinerary, to make my own markings on the map. Now I plan my trips with me in mind and leave the tours to the neophytes.

12. It sounds like there's plenty of room for innovation in working out a life strategy. How do I make sure I stay open to new experiences?

Of course, to plot your traveling—or your life— this way, you have to be willing to look around, to try new approaches, to invent. Several summers ago, en route to the ancient Incan city of Machu Picchu, I was stuck on a train for seven hours. Seven hours on a train to spend one hour at the ruins! Only when I got back from that grueling experience did I discover that I could have had a thirty-minute helicopter ride instead and taken aerial shots of the whole site besides. No one had told me there were helicopters, and I never bothered to investigate. I had accepted the conventional way of getting there.

Perhaps no one has told you there are helicopters either. Perhaps no one has ever told you that you were on a journey, or that, with practice, you could improve the quality of that journey. But to do this, you have to look around and explore unconventional possibilities.

13. To what extent can I prepare for the "journey" of my life?

Even Sir Edmund Hillary, one of the first men up Mt. Everest, began with smaller mountains, and went through considerable training and hardship before conquering "the roof of the world." The same principles that governed his preparation apply to the kinds of overwhelming experiences you are having right now. Because you haven't been trained to deal with them, you are uncomfortable with your reactions, fearful of dealing with the unknown and wary of tapping yourself rather than others for advice. With exercise, patience, and perseverance, all of that can change. I don't say you'll be able to scale a Himalayan peak tomorrow, but just taking that first step, that first walk outside to look around, is a healthy start.

From there you can look into helicopters.

3.

Stress and Its Mastery

1. I was brought up to believe that everything in our lives must happen naturally. Isn't it being manipulative and insincere to plan consciously how to behave or to respond to a situation?

Nothing could be further from the truth. In fact, few of us have the capacity, as the Beatles song put it, to "act naturally." To expect that going with your feelings will make everything come out fine is just wishful thinking. For one thing, your feelings are not simple and clear-cut—as you already know. For another, it often takes a great deal of conscious effort to figure out which of your many conflicting emotions are the most important in any given situation.

So even though I've said that you'd be better off if you learn to express your feelings rather than conceal them, I'm well aware that finding out what those feelings are can be a major task in itself. You can get your emotions and your thoughts under control, but it's not simply a matter of recognizing the real you and taking it from there. In a sense there is no real you; you are what you make of yourself each day.

2. How can I change the way I feel?

Basically, deciding on what to think about or how to cope with different situations is a matter of recognizing that your brain—no less than your arm or the way you comb your hair—is under your control. You can decide what you're going to think about and the way in which you're going to function. Leaving these processes to chance or to random impulses means giving up the right to use your intellectual and emotional gifts for your own good. Going with the flow, in other words, can be a quick way of doing yourself in. Learning how to choose what to think about so you can control your responses, on the other hand, can give you a sense of real confidence and keep you from being overwhelmed by the pressures around you.

It can also be a way of effecting change not only in yourself, but in those around you. This is an important point to remember since you may have the inclination when you are feeling disheartened and anxious to try to control the behavior of others by telling them what you want them to do or what you want them to stop doing. This rarely works and may be the source of considerable conflict. The only person you can change directly is you. But if you change your own behavior, you'll find that others will automatically begin to react differently to you, and this means, in effect, that you will have changed them as well.

3. How can I eliminate the feeling that I'm being trapped and controlled by others, with no free choice, free time, or free will?

That's a common and understandable feeling, but it's the result of an erroneous assumption: that other people have power over you even if you don't want them to. That is simply wrong. You *can* keep the world from stepping on your toes, and the way you begin is simply by controlling your own behavior. You can set limits on the extent to which you cooperate with other people's demands, spoken or silent. And you don't have to be a hermit in a forest. You can set limits no matter how intimately or constantly you are involved with others.

4. *Is it possible to prepare for stress?*

Definitely. To begin with, the more you control the smallest, most insignificant actions of your daily life, the less chance there will be of tension and depression building up within you, and subsequently the more control you will have. You *can* reduce the stress and tension in your life, but you've got to start small.

Take an example. When the Apollo astronauts were training for the moon shots, they knew that they would soon be subjected to levels of stress that few people in human history had ever experienced. No doubt that gave them many shaky moments. But they didn't deal with the problem, at the beginning, head on. That is, they didn't train specifically to confront the overpowering tension of lift-off or reentry or landing. What they did was to prepare themselves, physically and emotionally, in small ways. They learned to note when their blood pressure and breathing were abnormal, and they learned to become calm in the face of that. They learned to observe and then, gradually, to control the many physiological reactions that even minor stress elicits—so that by the time the real test came, they were ready. At lift-off their blood pressure and pulse rates were exceptionally high, but because of their training, they came through the mission splendidly. Because practice had taught them what was coming, they didn't panic. They were dealing, after all, with an unruly but well-known friend—their own stress responses.

5. *Can I learn to control my reactions to my own stress responses?*

If you learn first to observe your own stress responses as the astronauts did, you can then learn how to control how you react to them. Take a spot check of yourself. The next time someone yells at you or you feel neglected at a party, ask yourself, "How is my body feeling about this? Are my palms sweaty? Do I feel unusually hot or cold? Is my heartbeat normal or fast? How does my stomach feel?" Getting in touch with the basic physiological symptoms of stress can be a valuable prelude to assessing how to deal with them. If you can't even feel that your stomach is doing flips, you won't have a very good chance of getting it to slow down.

6. Once I recognize my physical stress symptoms, what steps can I take to learn self-control?

After self-observation, the important next step is self-control. "He who reigns within himself and rules his passions, desires, and fears," said the English poet John Milton, "is more than a king." The person who can learn to calm himself in the midst of misfortune or nervousness has a far better chance of success in all areas of life than the one who is prey to a thousand tricks and turns of emotion. This takes a bit of training and practice, to be sure, but any effort toward that end will be well worth your trouble.

I don't mean that you should lie to yourself or to others, pretending to be calm when you're not. In fact, that's just the opposite of what you want to do. What I mean is that, faced with a troubling or threatening situation, you should strive for balance and poise; you should hold off a bit before you lash out at someone who has offended you; you should think before either responding in anger, or retreating into sullenness; you should have enough confidence in your own sensibilities to temper your anxiety with reason, knowing that only you can bring clarity and patience into your view of the situation.

The tragedy, and the beauty, of human consciousness is, as the American poet Wallace Stevens said, that "We live in the mind." Many of us take this knowledge as a kind of curse and feel that we are doomed to be imprisoned in our own heads. But it need not be that way. Understanding the power of our subjective minds can, in fact, be a step on the road to psychological freedom. To some extent your thoughts determine both your behavior and the circumstances and events around us, and actually the kinds of experiences we have in the world.

7. How can I eliminate fear?

The person who constantly predicts defeat for himself often ends up, not surprisingly, in last place, while the person who habitually predicts success has a far greater chance of achieving it. This is an example of the self-fulfilling prophecy. Approaching things from a negative viewpoint, in other words, is like giving yourself two strikes before you even step up to the plate. The batter who enters the box convinced he can't do anything against the pitcher's famous curve will very likely end up striking out.

Are you reluctant to act because of a fear of

failing? I can understand that. We're all afraid of blowing it, of looking like fools in front of our friends. But why not consider a different view-point? Maybe it's precisely your unwillingness to act that ensures your continued failures. Maybe you've got the whole thing backward, and the only reason success has eluded you is that you've denied yourself that 100 percent effort that would bring it within your reach.

8. What can 100 percent effort do for me?

When you focus all of your energy on the task before you and waste none of it thinking about the outcome, you achieve unexpectedly gratifying results. In many endeavors, such spectacular results come only after you have pushed yourself beyond where you thought you could go. Like the marathon runner who gets her second wind just when she thought it was all over, you may find that success is simply a matter of a little extra try.

Most of us who fear failure do so out of an unnecessarily strong sense of defensiveness. Since we don't want people to laugh at us, we refuse to put ourselves in any situations where that might be a possible outcome. But by depriving ourselves of the chance to fail, we also deprive ourselves of the chance to succeed, and we end up risking—and doing—nothing. This puts us in a perpetual limbo.

9. What if I fail?

Many people don't try things because they are afraid they'll be embarrassed or look foolish or feel inadequate if they aren't instant successes. They refuse to run the risk of failing, forgetting that, no matter how capable they are, they are always going to run into situations that tax their resources beyond their limits and therefore set them up for a fall. In fact, the more successful you have been in the past and the more challenging your objectives now, the more, rather than less, opportunity you will have to fail in the future. That's just the nature of striving.

10. What can I learn from failure?

Failures can actually be a plus. They offer you a chance to learn and improve what you're doing, to look for new ways to accomplish what you want. Remember that winners are people who have failed many times but have learned from their defeats. As Wendell Phillips said, defeat is "nothing but education, nothing but the first step to something better." You can't really fail if you pursue personally meaningful goals. On the other hand, if you pursue the goals set for you by others, you may still feel frustrated and unfulfilled even if you achieve them. In other words, success per se will not be satisfactory for long unless it is linked to your natural abilities and interests, in which case you are likely to keep at something even if you do not succeed at first.

11. *Can I be the person I want to be despite my age and circumstances?*

You can reach a level of self-realization at any time, regardless of circumstances, age, or other factors that seem to limit you. Most people don't make it because they don't believe that they can become who they want to become and so they don't even try. But if you take stock of your dreams and begin to act on them consciously, they'll soon become part of your reality. In the process of turning dreams into reality, you'll become more competent, more knowledgeable, more centered, and more certain of yourself.

Remember that nobody is holding you back from your goals. Only *you* can hold you back, and you do this generally because of fear of looking foolish to other people. Keep in mind that looking foolish to others never lasts very long—think of all the politicians who began their careers as less than dynamic speakers and got to be outstanding. If you can learn to accept this kind of trivial discomfort for ten or twenty minutes at a time, it will pass, and you can get on to the business at hand. Practice timing the duration of those feelings of discomfort. You'll be surprised, I think, at how quickly they disappear when, instead of worrying about them, you simply observe them and let them pass.

Later I'll give you some specific hints as to how to go about this. Now, I'll just ask you to remember that life is a marathon, not a sprint. If no one has ever explained this to you, it's easy to think of yourself as a failure. But the journey is in front of you, not behind. Yesterday's results are history. If you believe at this point in your life that you are a success and can rest on your laurels, you are in far worse shape than one who has failed but is still goal-directed, because you have stopped growing and learning. The real key to success is resilience, the ability to bounce back from failure. Working with Olympic athletes for a number of years, I found repeatedly that the distinguishing mark of the real champions was their lack of a fear of failure. In fact, champions are stimulated by their failures. They learn from them how to go on with the race, at the same time that they learn not to be distracted by their successes.

You may already have failed at a number of things. You may even believe that life has passed you by and that there is no way you can make things work out right. That's an understandable but false perception. The truth is that you were simply unprepared for discouragements and setbacks, which could have happened to anyone. If you can visualize your life as a long-distance run, one for which you are continually revising your strategy, you can begin to think—and behave—like a winner. Nobody tallies up all victories and no defeats; the successes are the people who learn from the latter and go on.

12. I usually feel so bad when I fail I don't know how to look at the experience and learn from it. What's the first step?

You can gain valuable perspective on yourself from failure if you control your defensiveness. This means getting into the habit of tolerating uncomfortable situations and feelings, and at the same time refusing to blame other people for your discomfort. Most of us, when we feel down, look outside ourselves for a reason. Talking about bad feelings becomes an exercise not in expression, but in attack. If we're feeling lousy, we say to ourselves that somebody else (never ourselves) must be at fault.

You can see how destructive this can be to yourself. To counter the effects of this kind of bad habit—and it's a habit we all have—I developed a role-playing exercise for the Life Strategy Workshops. You can tell someone else how you feel without putting him—or yourself—on the defensive. This is harder than it sounds, but with practice it is possible to talk about your feelings without trying to justify them or attribute them to the person with whom you are talking.

Say, for example, that a friend has just dismissed your opinion of a new movie with the comment, "I think you missed the real point." Your first inclination might be to snap back. "That really ticks me off," you might say. "What the hell do you know about it, anyway?" Yet this would be merely another heated opinion and would only close off further conversation, or start an argument.

A better approach would be really listening to the other person and then trying to understand his viewpoint. You might ask your friend what the "real point" is, how he arrived at his opinion and so forth. By focusing on his views you will find yourself getting less defensive and more comfortable. Later, when things are relaxed, it may be possible to let him know that you were upset by his abrupt rejection of your opinion. It would be helpful to your relationship if you were both aware of the mutual effects you were having on each other. This might open communication between the two of you, but you must remember that such openness can be a delicate business since often it may put the other person on the defensive.

13. Won't I be more vulnerable if I talk about my feelings?

The first reaction is a defensive, automatic response designed to make yourself look better than the antagonist. The second reaction is a conscious attempt, however pained, to communicate—an open admission of your own vulnerability. You may not believe that your efforts to express yourself straightforwardly like this can make a difference, or that hostile reactions generally only trigger more hostile ones. I know it's easy to think that you can only be happy if you are right and someone else is wrong. But if you are to find your own way, you must set yourself beyond comparisons. Naturally, if you spend your time constantly comparing what you have with what someone else has or what you have achieved with someone else's accomplishments, you're going to be miserable. The medals are always shinier on someone else's chest. You want to strive for a situation in which you determine your own failures and successes, in which you use your own particular assets to the fullest measure possible, and in which your view of yourself is not contingent on anybody else's view of you.

You don't have to prove yourself to anybody. The sooner you realize this, the better you will begin to feel.

Maybe you think this is all nonsense. Maybe it doesn't explain the facts as you know them—the fact, for example, that some people have been getting straight A's from the first grade through grad school with no effort at all, or that other people, no matter how little they seem to work, invariably earn more than everyone else. You may even feel that, no matter how hard you try, you still won't be able to do what others are doing without effort.

Well, this may be true, but so what? The point is to discover what you do well, not to follow somebody else's footsteps or plans. And everybody does something well. It may take a little looking, but you can find it. But you won't find it very fast if you start out thinking you can't.

Here, the words of Emerson are particularly relevant: "Insist on yourself; never imitate. Your own gift you can present every moment with the cumulative force of a whole life's cultivation, but of the adopted talent of another, you have only an extemporaneous half-possession. That which each can do best, none but his maker can teach him."

14. *On what should I focus my attention?*

What I'm getting at is that changing your present circumstances is a matter of concentrating on efforts rather than results. Since we're pretty much obsessed with results in our culture, that's often very difficult. But it's the only path I know to the freedom that comes when you know that you are the one calling the shots.

I know it's easy to get discouraged, but, after all, everybody loses. Look at the experiences of famous athletes, actors, or writers. All of them have had more failures than successes. In fact, you can never count on success. What you can count on is your own ability to withstand things, no matter what the outcome. Developing the ability to roll with the punches, to laugh at yourself, to approach winning and losing philosophically rather than as a matter of life and death—these things in the long run will serve you far better than a single perfect performance for which you may have sacrificed your peace of mind.

15. How can I change habits I don't like?

You can maximize your chances of success by paying attention to another important aspect of change—that most of us live most of our lives by rote, but that it is possible to alter this by conscious preparation and planning. We may be creatures of habit, but no habit is unbreakable, and ultimately the critical issue for your happiness is your ability to shift out of your habitual patterns of response into a pattern that brings you greater joy, greater opportunity for expression. To do this, you have to be able to visualize your habitual responses in advance and become especially aware of the kind of situation that triggers a habitually anxious response.

Most people experience anxiety when they accede to the requests of others in order not to offend them or make them angry, even though they may be acting contrary to their own best interests. Well, since you know this kind of a situation almost always makes you uptight, why not plan for it in advance right now? Tell yourself that the next time this kind of thing comes up, you're going to do something different. You're not simply going to sit through it and suffer.

Say, for example, that you hate listening to a certain long-winded friend on the telephone, but have done so uncomplainingly in the past for fear of offending him. While it might not make things any easier for you to tell him, "Look, Joe, I think you're a bore and I wish you'd shut up," it will help if you begin by making a small change in the way you respond to the situation. You don't have to offend him, but you can make yourself feel differently about what is going on. Try, for example, to write down notes of what your windy friend says. The act of doing this will lead you to listen more carefully to what he is saying so that you can respond more appropriately. Moreover, by recording what he is saying rather than reacting immediately you are likely to have some influence on the way in which he continues to communicate, since he will be responding differently to the change in your behavior. Your own emotional reactions will not be intensifying his communications to you.

Writing things down may not make him any less wordy, but it will make what he says less oppressive to you, because writing it down will act as a distancing factor. In addition, you'll have something concrete to reflect on when you review the conversation with yourself later. Your notes could give you some insight into your own responses and why, specifically, you feel put upon whenever that particular friend calls.

16. Are you suggesting that changes in behavior can lead to a reduction in stress?

Yes. By altering an external habit, you may find that you have also altered the internal responses, the agitation and stress you have habitually associated with it. The philosopher William James, for example, was convinced that literally "whistling in the dark" could actually make someone less fearful of the dark. Far from being an act of false bravado, putting up a display of courage, in James's estimation, frequently led to the whistler's actually feeling more courageous.

Remember that when you are asked to do something you don't want to do, you always have the option of doing something else instead. And you can do this right now, right while the external circumstances of your life are exactly the same as they have always been. It's simply chasing phantoms to believe that everything will be all right as soon as you've dropped out of your present situation, moved to San Francisco, told everyone off, or gone into debt for a new car. It won't be. The only thing that can make things all right is your decision to change the way you react to the situations, good and bad, in which you find yourself.

That decision, of course, is only an initial step. Beyond that, you have to begin to set goals for yourself and move consciously and with determination to carry them out.

4.
Step-by-Step
Progress

*1. I seem to get off-balance very easily. What
can I do to become more emotionally stable?*

In recent years people in the human potential
movement have been talking about finding their
"centers" or "becoming centered" as a way of
achieving greater happiness and self-esteem.
What they mean by being centered is being so in
touch with their own needs and desires that the
opinions and urgings of others do not affect them
adversely.

When you've found your own emotional cen-
ter of gravity, you've found the capacity to keep
calm in the face of stress. So, like one of those
weighted dolls that can be pushed over and then
pops back up, you can pop back up when some-

body shoves you down. Being centered, you have a firm hold on your own sense of balance, you are in touch with the emotional and integrative centers of the mind, and have turned off the tendency to be hypercritical and overintellectual about yourself.

Now, achieving this happy state is not an overnight task; it takes time, and often a lot of hard work. But before you get discouraged about the prospect of accomplishing it yourself, you should know that there is one thing you can do right now to begin regaining your balance: set a goal.

2. That sounds simple enough, but I'm not exactly sure what you mean. How should I go about choosing a goal?

Setting new goals is never easy, especially if it's the first time you've been faced with this challenge recently—as might be the case if you just finished high school or were recently fired from your job, divorced, or widowed. The decisions you have to make are huge. If you lack a set of personal goals, if you have too many goals, or if your goals are too challenging or confusing, you can feel considerable anxiety no matter how good your choices look. The mere number and range of those choices can be truly bewildering, I know, and unfortunately I can't give you a neat prescription to make your decisions easier.

The best advice is to choose what you want to do, and what is within your reach, rather than following someone else's conventional idea of success. In other words, don't join a club, volunteer for some committee, or take up the guitar simply because they seem like the popular things to do. You know best what interests you. If you persist in pursuing someone else's dream, you're really only buying into a nightmare. Without even knowing your specific interests, I would guess that much of your distress is a result of the fact that until now you have been pursuing goals set for you by others, rather than those you have set for yourself.

3. *What guarantees are there that this will work?*

Again, I don't say that this is easy. Not only is it difficult to set reasonable, single-minded goals, but there is no guarantee, once you do set them, that the first one, or the tenth, will be realized the way you want. If you keep at it, though, you will achieve a goal, and then will be able to see your present suffering as so much preparation for that end.

4. Is it possible to write your own script?

Can you become chairman of the board, a Pulitzer Prize winner, an Olympic medalist? Maybe, maybe not. But you will only know if you begin by picking an attainable goal and taking the first steps; the goal itself is unimportant, but marshaling your now-dormant energies to choose one is significant. The day you pick a specific goal and start working toward it, you will begin to control your life.

It has taken me a long time to recognize the simple truth that the effort to reach a goal is more important than the goal itself. The virtue of goals is largely to challenge you, to bring out your best, to give you perspective and direction. Achieving the goal is not critical, though it can certainly be pleasant and rewarding. I emphasize this because most of the time when you are depressed you will feel defeated about not achieving certain goals, mistakenly assuming that they are critical for your peace of mind, when in fact they are only signposts to a yet unwritten future.

Even though inertia may be in charge now, selecting some goals, even if you aren't absolutely sure of your preferences, will help you get moving sooner. The important thing is to have an objective, no matter which one, to move toward. This is because changes are always easier to manage when you are in motion than when you are stalled.

> *5. Although I can see the value of choosing a goal, I hesitate because I'm afraid I may choose the wrong one. How do I get past this?*

I can't tell you specifically which goal is best for you, but I can tell you which *kind* of goal might be best. Generally speaking—and especially when you're depressed—it's best to start with a modest, achievable goal for the immediate future. Determine, for example, to spend a set number of hours studying a particular subject or practicing a sport or musical instrument, or visiting a friend, a museum, or some local historical site you have been planning to see for years. Leave off dreaming about moon shots for a couple of weeks; once your first, immediate goals are met, you can gradually work up to greater things.

6. *Are you saying it's best to start small?*

It's up to you, of course, but I'd strongly suggest that you not aim for the stars just yet. If you were a runner just getting over a case of the flu, you wouldn't start the first day back at practice trying to break the four-minute mile. You'd start slowly, and work up to the bigger achievements.

Once you set a short-term objective, keep track of your progress. Keep a notebook or just write down on scratch paper how much time you spend at your chosen task each day. Gradually try to increase the time spent, and this will build up your confidence and ability to achieve longer-range goals.

If you find yourself getting bored with the task you have set, perhaps it's time to make it more challenging: make it more complex or shoot for a higher level of performance. Experience will tell you which goals are challenging but attainable for you, and you can adjust your sights and efforts accordingly. Experience, too, will show you how hard you are willing to work for something, how distractible you are, and how you actually want to parcel out your time.

7. How many goals should I set?

Now, it's very easy, when we're setting out plans for ourselves, to scatter our shots so wide that we never get anything done. We may convince ourselves that our interests are too broad to be confined by a simple design, but actually this frequently becomes a way of avoiding the effort to finish any one task. As the Englishman Sir Henry Bulwer noted: "The man who seeks but one thing in life may hope to achieve it; but he who seeks all things only reaps, from the hopes which he sows, a harvest of barren regrets." You may not want to limit yourself to one goal, but unless you *start* with only one, you'll never get to the ten, or ten thousand, of which you may eventually be capable.

8. How specific should my goals be?

The more specifically you can define your goal, the easier it will be for you to establish priorities and determine what you are willing to do to make your reality conform to your dreams. This sounds simplistic, but it is true. Most people know what it takes to succeed in various endeavors, but are unwilling to make the sacrifices, run the risks, or do what it takes to become who they want to be.

9. *What exactly will a goal do for me?*

There's no magic involved in the connection between goals and contentment. Think of it this way. Having a goal will eliminate a basic frustration in your life, one of the major sources of your distress—your lack of purpose. Knowing where you are headed makes getting there that much easier.

For example, if you are a high school student, you may wish that school were over and you were already working at the job of your choice. Realistically you probably know that your prospects will improve once you have a diploma; even if you hate school you'll get through it better if you think of it as a necessary step toward your objective.

If you're stymied in your job, having reached the top of the promotion ladder in your company with no place to go, you may want to give serious consideration to a major career change, in the direction of pursuing dreams you were postponing until retirement. Maybe now is the time to go back to school or start that small general store you always dreamed of, or take that sailboat trip around the world.

Even if you're a senior citizen with some medical disabilities, there may still be plenty of room for revamping your life-style in line with long-suppressed wishes to do something extravagant—take a trip or even move to another city. There is always room for relinquishing certain burdens that have accumulated over the years and which you have been reluctant to abandon.

10. What steps should I follow to reach my goal?

Certain steps are essential for certain goals. If you want to go to graduate school, you'll have to finish college with good grades first. If you want to be a carpenter in Maine, you will have to learn about hammers and saws. Acquiring the requisite skills can be a real pleasure when you view it as preparation for attaining a desirable goal.

Having faith that you will reach your goal, you will be able to relax and function in a way that maximizes your assets. Instead of scattering your energy in many directions, distracted by the advice of friends and relatives, you will begin to focus on that narrower range of activities you do best.

I don't mean that you should immediately focus on a single objective and forget about all other interests. You couldn't do that even if you tried, and in fact sometimes it's a real advantage to be able to dream beyond that immediate goal. In the short run, give it all you've got. But in the broader perspective, don't be afraid to listen to your daydreams—especially the ones that seem impossible. Time spent in daydreaming and fantasy about the future can be extremely useful, particularly if you allow yourself the luxury of considering all of your thoughts, even the ones you think are ridiculous. Others may advise you to be more serious in your thinking, but it's you, not they, who know what you really want. Our society puts great stock in rational approaches to living, but the seed of most great achievements, whether on the gridiron or in the laboratory, is an unrealized and often impractical idea or daydream. Genius, said Thomas Edison, is 1 percent inspiration and 99 percent perspiration. You know that the sweat is important, but that doesn't mean you should forget about the other 1 percent.

11. How does Edison's experience relate to me?

You may be tempted to say that Edison was not typical. He was exceptional, and you are just an ordinary person. You can't be expected to achieve his kind of results, no matter how much you dream or work.

If you're thinking this, you should remember that Edison became exceptional; he wasn't born that way. And he achieved his success by following precisely the kind of advice I'm suggesting; he set himself a goal, and then worked to achieve it.

12. How will setting a goal affect my depression?

Pursuit of a meaningful objective is fundamentally of value not because of the significance of the goal itself, or because of the success you'll achieve because of it, but because it challenges you and brings out your own untapped abilities. This is why it is important to strive, because only then can you really test your limits and discover your strengths. The sooner you fix a goal for yourself, the more comfortable and ultimately satisfying your life will be, because when you set a goal, you develop a sense of mastery and control over yourself.

How much you accomplish relative to others doesn't matter. What matters is how high you strive relative to your *own* ability. Moving beyond your own base line will give you a sense of achievement and personal discovery, and it is of almost no consequence in which area of activity you choose to do that—as long as you select something that has meaning and significance for you.

All the feelings that are making you miserable—your sense of failure, lack of worth and recognition, resentment, and boredom—will start to fade away once you start making a real effort to pursue meaningful goals. As you know by now, you cannot get rid of these feelings by looking on the bright side. What you need is something to galvanize your energies away from morose reflection and toward self-approval. A goal will serve this function beautifully.

13. What's a good way to plan?

You can maximize your chances of fulfilling your objectives, moreover, if you remember my earlier advice about planning. Your plans do not have to be elaborate, but the clearer you are about what you want to accomplish, the more likely will be your success.

Sit down for a half hour each day with a pencil and paper. Write down all your thoughts about possible goals—everything you might want to accomplish or obtain or become. Try for three or four thoughts a day. Don't worry about how foolish some of them seem to be. This is for your eyes only. In a month you'll have about a hundred ideas to examine, and from these you can begin to discern a pattern of interests. Somewhere in that pattern will be one or more ideal immediate goals.

Go over your list and decide on one thing you want more than the rest. It may be a small thing—learning to swim, improving your tennis, earning some extra money, learning to play the guitar—or it may be a major objective like becoming an astronaut, getting a good job, going to California, becoming a salmon fisherman in Alaska, or getting your own apartment. Whatever it is, write your objective on a small piece of paper, carry it with you always, and start thinking every day about how to achieve it.

It might help to imagine that the goal is not your own but someone else's. Try thinking through how you would advise someone else who wanted to do the same thing. Stand back from yourself long enough to see what your advice would be to a friend aiming for your goal. Write that advice down, and step by step try to follow it. If you think about your goal every day, you will gradually find yourself overcoming the inevitable problems and obstacles along the way to achieving it.

14. *What else can I do to get into action?*

You can do life-plan exercises daily. Start each day with a set of objectives you want to accomplish that day. Maybe Monday you want to call about a photography course at the local camera store; Tuesday you want to investigate that job at the record shop; Wednesday you'll organize your closet; and so on. Keep a diary of everything you do—what happened, how you spent your time— and at the end of the day or week or month, you will be able to see whether you are spending enough time and effort on reaching your designated goal. This will give you some feedback, which you can then use to revise your planning and efforts.

15. *What if I can't achieve the objectives I have set?*

If you find you can't accomplish the daily objectives you set for yourself, divide your activity into smaller units. If you can't get moving at all, try setting your sights a little lower. If you're depressed, it's absurd to expect yourself to achieve what you would normally achieve. Your objective for the day might be simply to get up and go to the grocery store or cook yourself a steak. It could be to skim over some easy part of a course you're taking or to tackle the simplest, most mechanical part of a job. Sometimes planning just one activity per hour can be helpful. As you feel better, you can set more challenging tasks.

16. How often should I schedule my activities?

Plan your day, every day. Before you go to sleep at night, or first thing in the morning, set up the day's activities so you'll know what's ahead of you. When you plan before you have to act, you'll avoid indecision and the confusion of meeting too many choices each day. This will also help you keep focused on what it is you really want to do.

As you make your schedule, you should visualize the upcoming activities in your mind. Close your eyes, relax, and see yourself doing the things you've set out to do. Focus first on activities that are easy and that cause you the least frustration. That way, you'll be able to progress to harder things as the day goes on.

17. Is there value in reviewing the day's events?

When the day is over, you might want to review your progress before you go to bed. As the

Roman philosopher Seneca noted, if every night we "call ourselves to account our vices will abate of themselves if they are brought every day to the shrift." Going over your successes and failings each night is a way of keeping track of where you are, and what you still have to do to accomplish your goals.

18. How can I avoid getting overcommitted?

You can't do everything. If you overcommit yourself, if you take on more tasks than you're comfortably able to handle, you'll get yourself buried in responsibilities for which you don't have sufficient energy. You may end up unable to do anything at all because you are feeling so pushed. You've probably already been pushing and overextending yourself. And it hasn't worked so well. So back off for a while. Don't be intimidated by people who want you to do them tiny favors that take time away from your plan. You've been intimidated long enough, and you can afford to be selfish for a while—at least until things are moving more smoothly for you.

This is your life, after all. A real friend will understand that, and will know that there are some things you simply have to do for yourself before you can begin taking on extra chores.

You must understand that too. You must learn to take care of yourself. You must be willing to go it alone in pursuit of your objectives and not worry about the approval or the abuse of others.

19. What if I make mistakes?

Naturally you're going to make mistakes. You may fail to learn from the past, or review alternate ways of approaching problems, or consider all relevant variables when making your choices. You may find yourself moving on to whatever new approach comes immediately to mind rather than planning the next strategy carefully. Any of these things can lead to failure.

But so what? Edison failed plenty. We all have. Failure is no proof of worthlessness. Seen calmly, it can be a spur to further achievement.

When you're frustrated, it's easy to become anxious, and anxiety in turn can lead to confusion, bad planning, mistakes—and more frustration. That's why it's necessary sometimes simply to slow down, to wait before making that next decision, to ignore the flurry of advice around you and consider slowly and quietly what's best for you.

20. *What can I do to control my impatience?*

You may be so uncomfortable with indecision and so impatient that you act quickly to eliminate the anxiety of uncertainty. Quick decisions, however, frequently cause you more anxiety in the end. One of the most important, and hardest, things to learn is how to *tolerate* uncertainty and delay your responses when such a delay will help you come up with a better solution. By learning to live with temporary anxiety, you can work toward eliminating the real, long-range anxiety that has been bothering you for so long.

A basic principle to keep in mind here is that each moment offers you an opportunity to test new ways of behaving. What has happened up to now is history. It need not determine what you choose to do next.

21. *What's wrong with getting the opinions of others?*

Try to recall how you usually make a decision in a crisis. You may handle crisis situations extremely well because you have no time to consider the opinions of others or the possibilities of error. When not in a crisis, you may feel obliged to discuss your personal decisions with others, and this can simply confuse the issue. You may, in seeking advice, be trying to rationalize your own indecisiveness or creating alibis. It's always easier to blame others rather than yourself for inaction.

Sure. it's possible to reduce your anxiety by talking to others. But when you do this, you also reduce the chances of developing your own real confidence. In fact, you reinforce your dependency on others and set the stage for stress. If you become increasingly dependent on "expert" opinions, you will be reluctant to do anything on your own. The very act of seeking advice to make you feel more secure in your plans and decisions can, paradoxically, make you feel less secure. Step-by-step decisions, like the overall scope of your life, are ultimately *your* responsibility. If you do need help in getting going and want the advice of others, you would be well advised to seek the help of professionals such as your minister or family doctor, all of whom are trained in the art of helping others without being so heavy-handed as to discourage individual initiative or encourage dependency.

5.
Changing Roles and Relationships

1. Self-observation, planning, setting goals—these are all very well. But what you don't seem to realize is that other people make it really tough for me to concentrate on what I want. They're always criticizing me or telling me what to do. How can I change that?

Difficult as it is to admit to it, you have probably invited others to treat you this way. To the extent that this is so, you can change this pattern by changing your own behavior. Consider whether you have learned to play the scapegoat role so as not to disappoint their unspoken need for you to be dependent on them. Do you in some ways prove they are right—that you are not strong enough to decide matters for yourself? Do you, instead of explaining how you feel, hold it all inside, feeding right into the idea that you are uncooperative or moody, like a sulking little kid? Have you made things worse by going along with their definition of you?

2. What harm is there in compliance?

Compliance with the expectations of others and reluctance to express yourself can build up guilt and resentment in you, and the more you hold things in, the more the tension will continue to mount. This in turn may lead to an explosion, which will only aggravate the people around you further, because it will be evidence that you are not only dependent but uncooperative as well. Viewing the fluctuations in your mood as evidence not of confusion but of negativism, they may seek to quiet the anxiety it causes them by adopting a punitive or moralistic attitude toward you. When people don't understand your viewpoint, dreams, fantasies, or behavior, they often react as if it were "mad" or "bad," instead of recognizing that they are making judgments from their own limited perspective and not giving you space, not understanding you from your own unique point of view.

3. How do people typically react to problematic behavior?

People generally react in one of two ways to the emotional problems of those who are close to them. They may focus on overt behavior rather than on feelings, take a moralistic view and resort to criticism instead of considering whether or not they had any part in contributing to your problems by their responses and attitudes toward you. Impatient, confused, and guilty, they may demand that you simply change your ways, even though that may be beyond your immediate capacity.

On the other hand, they may go overboard in the opposite direction. They may become abnormally helpful and understanding in a way that actually minimizes the seriousness of your problems. Influenced by their own anxieties and by the erroneous belief that depression is always terribly stressful, they may go out of their way not to yell at you or make demands.

But whether they use the hard-line or the soft-pedal approach, they give evidence that they are out of touch with what you are really going through.

4. What effect can the attitudes and reactions of others have on me?

Whether you like it or not, people and especially close friends and relatives are extremely influential in determining how you feel. You may feel that you've grown so far away from people that they couldn't influence you even if they tried. Sometimes, this will tempt you to say, "The hell with them, I don't need anybody." That's an understandable reaction, but if you think about it, you'll see it's not really on target. Whether you view them as good or bad, as loving or unloving, as supportive or destructive, their influence on you is unavoidable. What you have to do is find a way to deal with it effectively.

You are no doubt trying to lead your own life, but this is hard to do when you're feeling depressed.

5. Why does it seem as if everyone is nagging me? Sometimes I think it is out of a perverse desire to make me miserable, but then again I doubt that. What's the real explanation?

Most people find it very painful to confront depression in someone they love, and they are frequently clumsy in expressing their concern. It may seem impossible to please them, but they may feel the same way toward you. Because they are just as anxious as you to be loved, they may overreact to your slightest criticism or mistake, concluding that there's no communication at all between you.

So the tension and feelings of rejection that you talk about may well be mutual. You're probably rejecting them as often as they're rejecting you. Sure, you crave special attention in this troubling time. But so do they.

I don't doubt that those who are close to you are less sensitive to you than you would like. But try to think why they might be acting like this. At this point in your life, they may have their own serious troubles. They may be going through their own crises.

6. How can I gain more objectivity about others?

You can begin by seeing others in perspective, as people with their own personalities, traits, virtues, problems, desires, interests, histories, faults, and fears. Remembering that you are not responsible for any of these factors will make it easier for you to be objective about them.

7. What's wrong in seeking advice?

Asking for advice is often asking for trouble. If the advisor tells you what you don't want to hear, *you* may get angry. And if you don't follow the advice, *he* may get angry. Advice-giving is a common cause of family arguments. Acting first, and then discussing the matter afterward, therefore, can often be a far better choice than asking for advice.

Acting as if you plan to follow someone's advice, and then doing just the opposite to demonstrate your independence, is pseudoindependence, a way of rejecting responsibility. This kind of behavior suggests that you are pushing loved ones to the limit to find out if they really care about you enough to tell you to stop. Most of us test people this way, and it very seldom has a good effect.

8. Sometimes I get really annoyed with the advice I'm given and have a tendency to lash out at others. Is this a good way of letting off steam so it won't build up?

Lashing out at somebody who is nagging or berating you often seems like the only reasonable thing to do. There's no doubt about it, anger is often the quickest response. But it's very seldom the best. So the first rule to remember when a fight is in the air is to disengage from the fray. Wait a moment before speaking. Listen to what they are saying. Try to understand the other person's point of view. Focusing on what he has to say will reduce your own inclination to be defensive. Not only will you not feel badly, but the other person will calm down too, and may even appreciate your attentiveness.

In the long run everyone will be the better for this, and you will not feel so compelled to prove your independence by "not taking any guff from anyone," an attitude that reflects dependence on the other person's opinions.

9. Are you advocating passivity?

No, I'm just suggesting that confrontations generally make matters worse. Argument breeds argument and leads to further conflict and demands—especially if others are worried about you. Don't feed their anxiety by doing and saying things you know very well will only set them off.

10. How am I disguising my dependency?

You may be letting others take responsibility for areas of your life that are really yours to control.

You may, having involved them in your decision making, express surprise that they fail to treat you as an independent, self-sufficient person. Since dependency can be disguised in many ways, you may be asking them for advice without even realizing it. When you tell people all your plans, for example, you invite their approval or disapproval. If someone disapproves of your plans, whether you grudgingly cooperate or angrily rebel, you have already included him in your decision. Recognizing this, you should be able to take responsibility for your requests. The best course may be to abide by the judgment you have invited, and the next time, keep your plans to yourself.

11. How can I become more self-reliant?

Learn to decide as much as possible for yourself, and in time you will know when it is best to rely on the judgment of others and when you can rely on your own. Of course, not all your choices will be good ones. But no one's choices can always be right, either, and it's far better to act on your own bad choice than on somebody else's possibly good one. Putting pressure on others by asking them to decide for you is a way of maintaining the very dependency you say you resent. Until you stop constantly testing the waters for approval, however, you will not learn to take responsibility for yourself.

Learning to keep your own counsel, to trust your instincts, and to act accordingly, is never easy. But this is your life, after all. Ultimately you are on your own, and the sooner you can learn to make your own decisions, the sooner your friends and relatives will accept the fact that you can in fact manage without them. When you complain that you're not getting their permission to do what you want, you're saying that you feel like a disgruntled child. If that's how you present yourself to them, that's how they're going to treat you.

It's hard enough to figure out what you want. Why complicate the issue by adding in the expectations and demands of others? Even if they're similar to your own, once you learn to follow your own advice first, you and those close to you will be relieved. Believe me, they don't like breathing down your neck any more than you like it, but at the moment they feel they've got to control your life, because you're not doing it yourself. As your behavior changes, their anxiety will diminish, and they'll learn to stop acting on your behalf.

12. Why is it so uncomfortable to be self-reliant?

If you aren't accustomed to choosing for yourself, the realization that you're the one in charge of your life can be overwhelming. When you take charge of yourself, you automatically give up that nice warm feeling of support you had during childhood, when you were sure your parents would take care of you and come up with all the right answers. This can make you feel lonely and anxious, and sometimes it can even aggravate family tensions. But that's temporary. Learning to ride out the discomfort and anxiety of acting on your own, without the approval of others, is one of the intensely exciting tasks of life. "The best government," the German writer Goethe observed, "is that which teaches us to govern ourselves." The more you can learn to rely on yourself, ultimately the less complicated your life will be.

13. Are you suggesting that I keep some things to myself?

Yes. Honesty is essentially a great policy, but that doesn't mean that you have to make everyone a confessor, rightfully privy to your every whim and fancy. When you are open about everything, you invite criticism and pressure. Learn to parcel out your confessions judiciously. Complaining every time you feel down will just send everyone up the wall, because it will make them feel guilty and responsible. Remember that your feelings, no less than your behavior, are your responsibility too.

Now, I can't guarantee that, if you practice the kind of understanding, judicious silence, and self-reliance I've been talking about, you'll never have another flare-up with anyone. No matter how cautious you are, occasionally you're still bound to feel put upon, and that feeling is going to push you to the breaking point.

14. What do I do if I reach the breaking point?

If you reach the breaking point, try out a technique I've found very useful for defusing antagonism. It's simply to *delay your responses.* You don't have to delay them for long; a few minutes will do. But fight the urge to blow up the moment you first see red. The most common automatic reaction to pressure—a display of anger—can often cause more problems than the pressure itself. Remember that you don't have to defend yourself or make decisions under fire. When you are critical or people make demands of you, don't react immediately; if you're pressed for an answer, tell them you'll let them know as soon as you can. Wait until things cool down and then decide.

Confrontations are rarely of value. They frighten you and everyone else, and you may all become more demanding because each of you fears losing control of the situation. Even if you do gain a point by fighting, you may feel uneasy about your victory because it came as the result of an unfriendly conflict.

15. Won't people be upset if I delay my responses?

Delaying your responses, I realize, may go very much against the grain of your usual interactions with others. Especially in families, people generally relate to each other in fixed patterns, with each person playing an expected role. Conflict is often built into the normal patterns. You'll be amazed, though, once you become aware of your own fixed-role patterns, how you can change them simply by taking some time out and refusing to act automatically, like a robot.

Think back to what I said about taking notes instead of reacting peevishly to that verbose friend on the telephone (page 54). You can use a similar technique in direct, face-to-face communication. Take mental notes. Review for yourself what is said and what is decided. Ask your friends or relatives to do the same, and compare notes with them. Problems frequently come up when two people forget what they said and have different versions of a single conversation. You can avoid this problem by consciously comparing versions.

This means, of course, that you and those close to you must learn to listen to each other. You can resolve a lot of problems if you can discuss the issues instead of adopting a defensive posture and yelling. Sometimes you need their feedback, so ask for their thoughts and give them a chance to analyze what's going on. This is not the same thing as asking for advice. It's just a way of getting all the information you can about the situation before deciding what you think about it.

Some of the information they give you may not be pleasant to hear, but you should welcome it anyway.

Sometimes criticism given in a calm, deliberate attempt to clarify a situation can be more useful than praise. Observations about your shortcomings, as Francis Quarles noted, can be either just or unjust, but either way they are useful. "Make use of both," he counsels, "so shall thou distill honey out of gall, and out of an open enemy make a secret friend."

16. How can I change the responses of others to me?

By asking thoughtful questions, paying attention to the answers, quelling your anger, and attempting to understand, you will make relations with others much easier than they have been up to now. Once people see you are taking them seriously and not just trying to buck them, they won't have to come on so strong. If you talk quietly and sincerely, without belligerence, you'll see a difference in their response. Most people want to be treated as individuals with importance and dignity, and tricky as it sometimes is, you can learn to do this without surrendering control of your life.

6.

Friendship and the Development of Self-Reliance

1. How do I set myself up for problems?

What I've been saying applies to all your relationships with relatives, friends, colleagues, and the like. While relatives are probably the worst offenders against your sense of personal integrity, your friends and even your casual acquaintances can also get in your way far more than is healthy for you if you let them. Among human beings, there is never a shortage of people who would prefer to run other people's lives rather than their own, and they'll readily make things tough for you even while they seem to be offering help.

But—and it's an important *but*—they'll do this only if you let them. If other people, as you say, are imposing on you, that's probably because you subtly invite them to do so. You know that your behavior influences the behavior of others toward you, so if you are constantly getting into arguments, for example, you might do well to find out if you are setting yourself up for them.

2. What kinds of things do I do that I can change?

Do you do anything that makes people free to impose on you? Do you smile and look agreeable when someone asks you for a favor—and then grumble in private? Is there something in your attitude or manner that leads other people to reject or annoy you? Do you check everything out with others before you act? Do you tell others everything you do so they can tell you what they think of it?

3. Are you suggesting that I am creating stress for myself?

Yes. In fact, you may be creating your own stress even in situations where others seem to be the cause of it. It's always easier to blame others, but as the medieval monk St. Bernard pointed out, "Nothing can work me damage except myself.

The harm that I sustain I carry about me, and never am a real sufferer but by my own fault."

I'll give you a specific example. Suppose you're working with someone who is a goof-off, and you feel you'd be under less pressure if only he would share more of the routine tasks and not leave you with all the extra work. Everything would be fine, you think, if your co-worker were more cooperative.

Having him cooperate more sounds like a good idea, but do you act as if you think that's a real option? Or do you do his work for him, complaining all the while? If you're taking up all the slack, there's no real reason for him to work harder. If you cover for him like this, you're operating not as an individual, but as part of self-perpetuating system that sustains both his indolence and your resentment.

A wise approach, in this kind of situation, might be not to tell your colleague off, but simply to let certain tasks go by the boards. Maybe, if you let certain things go undone, he might see the need of his increased cooperation. You would be running the risk, of course, that things would not work out to your satisfaction, but at least you wouldn't continue to feel responsible and resentful at once. And it couldn't make matters much worse, could it?

4. Are you suggesting that I not assume responsibility for others?

Exactly. The point I'm making is that you never do yourself any good by taking on other people's tasks grudgingly. If you like the extra work, fine. If not, you're only putting yourself in a martyr role, probably to cover up feelings of personal inadequacy. This can only undercut you, because martyrdom feeds all too readily into the familiar pattern of resentment, repression of feelings, guilt, and more resentment. We've already seen what a mess that can get you into.

I'm aware, of course, that to some extent society does contribute to your dissatisfaction and stress. As long as you live with other people, there will be some conflict between how you behave and how others feel you should behave. No matter how hard you try, you're bound to keep running into people who will try to pressure you into behaving their way rather than your own. That will lead to conflict, misunderstanding, even broken friendships and separations.

5. How about more personal relationships? They seem to be full of problems.

All the difficulties of communicating with other

people are aggravated in close relationships, especially romantic ones. Whether you are a teenager, a recently divorced forty-year-old, or a senior citizen embarking on a new romance, the fewer experiences you have had in the past, the more overpowering these difficulties can seem. The confusion about relating to other people in general can be bad enough; when you compound that with all the bewildering little twitches of sexual attraction, the result can be devastating. Although, ironically, any experiences with love and separation will prepare you for later experiences, I know they can often seem like nothing so much as an unending bad dream.

Romantic love can be awfully confusing because standards of conduct and norms of behavior are not only mixed but rapidly changing. Concerns about finding oneself, which begin in adolescence, coupled with a fear of being exploited and the uncertainty of acceptance, often persist throughout life, causing confusion for many. This is especially true when it comes to the differences between love and sex, between love and friendship, and between the different ways in which men and women seem to think, almost as if they had been raised in different cultures.

6. What makes relationships work best?

The important thing to remember here is that relationships, sexual or otherwise, generally work best when both parties have a common objective and a common outlook on life. Falling in love is never enough; the relationships that last are formed by people who share things. That, I'm afraid, is part of the reason that so many marriages fail; they're made not in heaven, as the partners seem to think, but here on earth between people who are still uncertain of what they really want out of life. All too often they discover, after the honeymoon, that they have nothing in common but a rapidly fading idea about being in love. At the first real conflict, they find out to their chagrin that the hearts-and-flowers folks were wrong. Love does *not* conquer all.

7. Is romantic strife inevitable?

Romantic strife is inevitable simply because it's hard, in the best of circumstances, for human beings to accept each other—accept their differences, I mean, as well as their likenesses. Once you discover your soul mate has a blemish, the temptation is to wipe it out and make him or her over into the perfect partner once again. Naturally this causes trouble, because few people want to be made over into another's image, no matter how much they like you.

It takes a while to learn not to try to change others over into your conception of how they ought to be. When you are on the receiving end of such attempts, you may find yourself going along, though resentfully, and to counterbalance your submission, becoming bossy and demanding. Conversely, when you make demands and others fail to respond satisfactorily, you also feel resentment. This pattern of alternating bossiness and submissiveness reflects an excessively dependent and unstable relationship that is likely to end abruptly, leaving everyone feeling devastated.

8. What happens when a relationship breaks up?

You're likely to feel devastated and ambivalent about whether to try to establish a close relationship with anyone else again. Because of your natural fear of rejection, you're wary of taking the initiative and at the same time annoyed by those who approach you. What can you do about this?

Well, it may seem paradoxical, but the first

principle to follow in building up your capacity to relate to others is that old standby self-reliance. Especially after a breakup. A breakup sometimes can be a blessing in disguise, in that it impels you to reexamine your own life, to demand of yourself that you begin to take care of your own needs, since no one else (apparently) is willing to do it for you. Only when you can do that will you be able to love freely, without the burden of needing someone to tell you you're okay.

9. Am I alone in feeling confused about sex?

No. For young and old people alike, relationships with the opposite sex, very difficult to establish in the best of conditions, are frequently aggravated by an abundance of confusing sex drives, especially during adolescence when within a relatively short space of time you can go from having no interest in the opposite sex to the discovery that you have a big effect on them, and they on you—and you don't quite know what to do. Distress about the power that some people now seem to possess over you no doubt accounts for the impact of the rejection.

10. How can I cope with the hurt that always seems to follow the breakup of a romantic relationship?

I have no sugar pills to help anyone get over the hurt of a thwarted romance, and I'm certainly not going to minimize its intensity. But it might help you to know that, even when a relationship is ended, the experience with it can always be illuminating and helpful to you in the future. Corny as it sounds, it *is* better to have loved and lost than never to have loved at all—not because it's morally right but because it widens the scope of your sensitivity, your ability to continue to grow.

11. What are the hazards of closeness?

The excitement and beauty of love can trigger tremendously positive forces in you, among them the capacity to be open and vulnerable to others. It can make you willing for one of the few times in your life to share that life with another person. That's no mean gift. It's so powerful, in fact, that when thwarted it can easily turn into rancor or envy or regret. Yet what links these emotions is an unrealistic attraction to lost causes. You can profit from your broken heart, but only if you first feel the pain—and then go beyond it.

You know now that it's only from others that you can discover certain hidden facets of your own character and personality; it's only in loving contact with other people that you enrich and broaden yourself. At the same time, though, the experience has left you feeling wasted and used up. This is an unpleasant paradox of love.

If you are willing to talk about your feelings, that's really terrific, believe me—even if you still feel vulnerable. For if you closed yourself off to protect yourself entirely, you might have felt relieved temporarily, but in the end you would have stopped growing as a person, and that wouldn't have made you feel good at all. You would have become like the anodyned, terrified character in the song, "I am a rock, I am an island," because a rock feels no pain, and an island never cries. It's really a plus, therefore, to still be feeling the pain.

12. What can I do when a close relationship comes to an end?

You may truly believe that you won't be able to continue living when a close relationship ends. You may say, with the country singer Skeeter Davis, that it's the end of the world. But when you think about it soberly, you know that's a notion based on a false appraisal of the world. In spite of any songs you *can* go on living without him or her, and you *will*. Which is why you really should be envied not pitied. If you've just experienced the breakup of a close relationship, you've just learned one of the greatest lessons of your life. You should be grateful enough for that to take a good look at it and see how it can help you in the future.

13. *Must separation be a part of every close relationship?*

Love and separation are experiences you must go through in order to develop the capacity to have close relationships with others. If you avoid such experiences in order not to be hurt, you will fail to develop the capacity to have such experiences, and that will severely limit your potential richness as a person. The more experiences you have of loving, the better you will behave in the future. Sadly, there is no way of developing this capacity without risk. But no great lesson is cheap.

You probably felt very much alive when you were in love. I can understand this, but wasn't there also a large amount of wishful thinking and dependency in your relationship, as well as a belief that, if you only let things alone, they would work out by themselves? Maybe you took drowsy infatuation for awakeness, and you've only now awakened from the dream.

It is difficult to learn that love flourishes most when you are least dependent on it, and withers when you desperately need it. People who can't live without each other generally are involved in very limited and eventually self-destructive relationships. For love to grow and evolve, you have to be able to get along without it. This is another crucial paradox.

14. Why do relationships hurt so much?

Partly because of the false assumption that you need the other person, partly because of ego, partly because openness followed by separation—even amicable separation—is experienced as rejection. Separation reactivates all our old feelings of guilt and unworthiness and self-blame. No wonder breaking up makes us feel lousy and not cared for by someone to whom we want to be close.

When this happens, you feel as though you don't fit in anywhere. If a lover or just a friend rejects you, it's hard to have confidence that anyone else will accept you. But consider what you might be doing to keep things on this unsteady ground. Remember the old monk's observation, "Nothing can work me damage except myself," and think about how you relate to others rather than how they relate to you.

What's wrong with most relationships is a tendency to pretend to share with others when in fact one's real feelings are kept to oneself. If you feel bottled up, it may be your hand on the cork. Maybe you try to protect yourself from people out of fear that they might hurt you as you were hurt in the past. Maybe you react to others as if they're only symbolic recapitulations of something in your past. The repetition of past patterns and the constraints of habits and predetermined life scripts may all be contributing to your problems.

What I'm suggesting is that you may be trying to fit into molds that are familiar to you—uncomfortable, perhaps, but known. Part of the reason you may feel blocked off from others is that they don't feel like reliving your life for you. They've got their own pasts—and presents—to contend with. They have no patience with someone who is by turns friendly and sulky, compliant and bossy, superficially open and guardedly closed, which is the way you are likely to be if you are depressed.

15. How can I improve my relationships?

If you try to accept the people around you as different from you, without trying to manipulate or change them, you may have better luck. At the same time, of course, you should make every effort not to allow them to control you, either. The key is to improve your communications by being more honest about your feelings—this means the bad ones as well as the good ones—and the ways in which you communicate.

We're all part of a vast communications network, a system in which you trigger responses in others, which in turn trigger responses in you, and so on. In effect you, unwittingly perhaps, instruct others as to how you want them to interpret what you say to them. Because this is so, you must be sensitive to the tone of your own voice, and to your attitudes, not just to the actual syllables you utter.

The development of your relationships with others is a delicate process, and most people usually don't realize how delicate they are. Nor how malleable. That is to say, most people do not consider the possibility of applying rational thought to their relationships in order to adjust and improve them. I realize this goes against the common notion that love is irrational, but you can actually learn quite a bit about yourself by coolly observing your typical interactions with others. You can also learn to control the way you present yourself, by modifying not only your actual words, but your style of saying them.

16. What should I look for in my own actions and attitudes?

Remember what I said about taking notes on your conversations? Those notes need not be limited to verbatim accounts of who said what to whom and when. They can include facial expressions, tones of voice, and your own feelings at the time of the interaction. All of this can be very useful when you sit down to analyze your own personal style of communication.

If, for example, you note that you said, "I'll be happy to lend you five dollars" to a friend, you have a record of only one level of discourse. If, however, you also note that, while you were saying that, you thought, "This son of a bitch hasn't paid back the two I lent him last week," then you have some insight into a deeper level of significance. In this particular instance, you know that you've held an angry response in check for fear of embarrassing yourself or your friend. That would be useful to remember the next time a similar situation arises.

This brings us back, of course, to a point I've already emphasized—that you can cause yourself enormous trouble by constantly suppressing your feelings. The containment of feelings more than anything else creates feelings of anger and resentment. Doing things you don't want to do in order to please others is bound to make you resentful, and covering up the anger that's generated by such compliance only intensifies the resentment and sets into motion the old cycle of repression, guilt, and more resentment.

17. What do you suggest I do to get rid of bad feelings?

Learn to examine your feelings. It will give you greater strength. Although feelings of fear, anger, and loneliness are terribly unpleasant, you should allow yourself to experience them in order to learn to neutralize them. The greater your awareness of what you are feeling, the greater your control.

The more organized and disciplined you are about this, the better. That's why I suggest you make a list of the ways in which you are frustrated by demands imposed on you by others and by your own inclinations to go along with this bad script. Every entry on the list should contain the answer to one or both of two questions: "What am I doing that I really don't want to be doing?" "What would I like to do and what's keeping me from it?" Study the list periodically, and start getting rid of the entries.

Of course, it's not easy to classify everything you do in terms of what you want to do and what you don't. Sometimes your feelings will be mixed. You may love your grandmother or your mother-in-law or a grandchild very much, yet not want to visit her on Sunday. You may enjoy your job but find you can't stand your boss. There will always be situations beyond your control, but you can learn to tolerate them if you try. By at least recognizing how you feel about the situation and why, you may be able to ride it out. Don't fight it out. Just let it flow around you, until it passes.

18. What should I learn to avoid?

You can also learn to avoid those specific situations that bother you most. You can learn to keep the world off your back, and to reduce the pressures around you. When you recognize the traps, you can start bypassing them, and live in a more selfish way.

I don't mean that negatively. What I'm talking about is not really selfishness but self-directedness. You don't owe your friends a shot at solving problems that you can solve much better yourself. The faster you cut down on soliciting their advice, the quicker you'll cut down the confusion and bad feelings that often come with such solicitation.

It's probably not advisable to discuss a breakup with "interested" or "concerned" friends. Not that they won't feel for you, because they probably do, but they may be too close to you to advise you sensibly, and it's certain also that their interpretations will be colored by their own histories, which may not relate very well to yours. You do not have to tell visitors or curiosity seekers about your experiences. No matter how loudly you hear it proclaimed that you should share your insights, you should share what you want and nothing further.

How can you tell whether to talk to a specific friend? Simple. Just consider whether you feel better or worse after discussing personal matters with him or her than you did before. When you feel enriched by communicating with someone, go ahead. When you feel threatened or bossed around, it's probably better not to talk.

What I'm suggesting is not simple. Essentially I'm saying that you have to walk a tightrope. You must learn to behave openly and honestly without being so blunt that you invite hostility from those around you. You must learn to be open without being cruel. At the same time you must learn that you don't have to explain anything, if you don't want to, to anybody.

In other words, keep your own counsel. While being open with your feelings, don't feel obligated to confess or reveal all your deepest secrets.

That doesn't mean you should sink deeper into the shell. On the contrary it means you should keep trying all the harder to reach out to people, but do so in a way that is not seen as threatening or abrasive. To treat them the way you probably would like to be treated yourself—with both honesty and kindness.

7.

Taking Charge of Your Life

1. It seems to me that I have more stress in my life than most other people. Is there a way to cut down on stress?

If you want to cut down on stress, you have to concentrate on what *you* do to bring that stress about. It may be unpleasant for you to hear that the problem is chiefly in your hands, but if you look at it objectively, that's a reassuring rather than discouraging notion. If you've essentially caused your own grief, then you can also get rid of it by yourself. There are no unseen, mysterious outside forces conspiring to keep you unhappy. There are usually no evil people out to do you in, although certainly there may be at times some cruel or misguided or even troubled friends, relatives, mates, or parents who may complicate your life. But even then, by recognizing that part of your problem which you are creating for yourself, you will be in a better position to begin to change it.

What I hope this book helps you realize is that, in a host of subtle ways, you complicate your own life a lot more than other people or circumstances have. In dozens of ways you put yourself into no-win situations. Conversely, you can use your own untapped psychological resources to increase your sense of satisfaction and eliminate the things that have been making you miserable. Since your world is a reflection of your innermost thoughts, you can change the impact of external events on you simply by changing the way you view them.

2. I sometimes think I give off vibes or something that asks for rejection. Does that ever happen?

It's not uncommon to feel rejected, to feel that people just don't understand you or want to try. That's a valid feeling. And if you feel that way, try to go one step further, and ask yourself whether you set yourself up to feel this way. Maybe you've been anticipating rejection by walking around with a chip on your shoulder, thus inviting people to respond to you negatively. Maybe you've been misperceiving the intentions of others by taking their statements literally instead of listening to the *way* they communicate with you. A friend, thinking of you as a strong and confident person, may make a joke at your expense without realizing how it upsets you—but if you don't let him know how you feel about it, you can't very well lay all the blame for your bad feelings at his door. People will treat you as you indicate you want to be treated.

3. I'm not sure about this, but I think I may be driving other people away. Could I be doing that?

You can't count on others to read your mind. You may think of yourself as shy, but you shouldn't be surprised if some people interpret your withdrawn attitude as evidence of snobbishness. Remember that rejection works two ways, and people may be just as afraid to approach you as you are to approach them. If you perceive this as rejection rather than evidence of their sensitivity, none of you will ever get very far in communicating.

It's natural for you to be withdrawn and skeptical now, but skepticism can cause you to overintellectualize and make incorrect assumptions about people's attitudes. That's why you should examine your own behavior periodically, and ask yourself what others see when they look at you. If you are so sensitive that you see threats to your self-esteem everywhere, you may be accusing others of a malevolence they don't possess. This is bound to frighten many people away. And it's something you can avoid by learning to examine things more objectively.

Dealing with other people is sometimes tricky. You have to be aware of what effect your behavior has on them, without being so influenced by their reactions that you forget who you yourself are. It's difficult to manage—so difficult, in fact, that all of us sometimes like to retire to the safety of our own rooms and retreat from the confusion of all relationships.

4. Do you mean it's okay to withdraw like that? I thought solitude was bad for you?

No. It's not necessarily bad. Sometimes taking a breather from other people is just what you need. Like many of us, you probably need to develop not only your capacity for communication, but your capacity for being alone. Sometimes being by yourself is the only thing that will increase your confidence in yourself and your capacity for self-reliance.

The earlier in life you can get some experience in handling solitude, the more satisfactorily things will go for you later on. Solitude gives you perspective, the capacity to make your own judgments, and the confidence that you can pursue your own objectives without the fear of ridicule.

When friends or relatives pressure you to respond to their demands or to explain yourself, solitude is often the best way to tap into your own feelings. Remembering how much clearer you were about your feelings when you were last alone can also help you get a handle on your emotions and eventually reduce your nervous reactions to pressure.

5. Sometimes I like being alone but sometimes it gets to me. Is there a reason for that?

It takes a certain amount of experience and practice to learn to be comfortable with solitude; without practice, those feelings of aloneness can easily turn into feelings of loneliness, which is not at all the same. Most of us grow up with people constantly around us, and in this country there's a strong cultural bias that being with others is desirable and being alone is bad. That's why loneliness and aloneness are often confused; it's hard to discover many of your talents when so many books, TV shows, and friends are telling you that you need others to find out who you are. Thoreau said he "never found the companion that was so companionable as solitude," but that's very easy to forget.

6. What are some of the benefits of solitude?

The more you learn to rely on yourself, the more satisfactory things will be for you. This is especially true, paradoxically, when it comes to relating to other people. The person who desperately needs external evidence of his worth is much less likely to get along well with others than the person who trusts his own intuitions and designs. Solitude can enhance self-confidence, and it's self-confident people who relate best to others. So you may have to limit the time you spend in personal relationships in order to pursue your relationship with yourself more fully. You should strive to find those activities that give you the best sense of yourself, that enable you to feel good about being who you are. This takes considerable effort, but in the long run it's worth it, because it can help you reduce the tension you feel when you choose not to live up to the demands of others.

7. Are you saying that I can build my own confidence? Be more in control?

Yes. What I'm talking about is a form of consciousness raising. Until now, most of what has happened to you has happened without too much awareness or deliberation on your part. Your life has been swirling about you, tossing you this way and that like a wood chip in rolling surf. But it need not remain that way. You have the power to control your own mental processes, and the more aware you become of these processes, the greater your chance of gaining control over your life. To the extent that you can modify your thinking, you can influence what happens to you. Maybe this sounds mystical, but it's really just common sense. "Mind over matter" is not just a guru's game; it's accessible to every one of us, every day.

8. You make it sound pretty easy to change, but aren't early childhood experiences important in determining the way I think?

I don't want to give you the idea it's easy. There is no question that patterns set in childhood have a way of holding on tenaciously, and some of these patterns can put a terrible crimp in your style. They can interfere with your starting to make decisions necessary to taking control of your life.

Decision-making patterns tend to be based on personality and history rather than on reason, and often lead you to repeat past "solutions," even if they haven't worked for you before. If, for example, you follow the lead of others in searching for the best course of action, you'll continue to have trouble developing decision-making skills. Most likely you do that simply because you're afraid your own decisions will be wrong. An unrealistically low opinion of yourself will make you reluctant to risk failure, and at the same time prevent you from seeing what possibilities are really available to you. But this is something you can change.

You have to learn to be more straightforward in making your own decisions and not worry so much about what others will think. This means that you have to develop the ability to choose wrongly and go on. Right now, because of a strong desire to please others, you sometimes may accept their views against your own better judgment, and then are even more confused when you still get blamed if it turns out to be a mistake. Ultimately you are responsible, even when you take other people's advice. That's one good argument for making your own decisions.

9. But some decisions just seem impossible to make, and I get into a panic. What can I do to avoid this?

If you have an inclination to be overcautious, it will lead you to examine every alternative and weigh every consequence before making a decision. This can contribute to your inability to act. If you are this afraid of being wrong, you can turn everyday situations into paralyzing moral and ethical dilemmas. Sometimes this can lead you to act impulsively, even explosively, in order to get over the discomfort of indecision as fast as possible. In effect you can be so caught up with the small issues involved in decision making that you lose sight of your major objectives. Maybe you can understand, then, why people so often seem exasperated with you. They're simply tired of waiting for you to make up your mind and annoyed that you seem to view every little thing in your life as a matter of life and death.

So we've got another vicious circle. Afraid of being wrong, you decide not to decide until the last minute. At that point you make a hasty choice, which proves as wrong as you feared it would in the first place. No wonder you mention panic, confused thinking, and clouded memory. This can be a typical reaction to your problems with decision making. You examine the same point over and over, like a needle stuck in a groove. Even your past experience cannot guide you, because your panic cuts off access to your memory. You're in another no-win situation.

But you can get out of it.

10. Do you have any concrete suggestions that can help me master such no-win situations?

There are several mental exercises that I use in the Life Strategy Workshops to get blocked people moving again toward making their own decisions. Maybe some of these exercises will help you.

The first one is simply to experiment with the word "no." Try saying no to someone to whom you typically respond with a yes. Try canceling an appointment or postponing a meeting. Try refusing some food at the table. Try not lending your notes to the friend who regularly borrows them.

More than likely, one or more of these actions will make you feel uncomfortable, because you're not used to doing things you know will make others uneasy with you (although you may already be doing them unconsciously). Persist in the exercise anyway. See how it makes you feel. Observe yourself getting upset. Bring your bad feelings to the surface and confront them. You'll be surprised how much easier it is to feel bad when you are making a conscious effort to do so. That's a first step in mastering the negative emotion that so far has been mastering you.

11. Are there any other exercises for controlling thoughts and bad feelings?

A popular second exercise, sometimes called "the empty jar," may seem silly at first, but it works. Sit down in a soft chair, close your eyes, get relaxed. Now, take three deep breaths, let them out slowly, and simply visualize an empty, un-capped jar. Then visualize yourself placing in the jar all your negative thoughts, attitudes, and expectations. Put them in one by one, observing and feeling each one as you do. Put in all your unrealistic expectations of affection, love, re-spect, and gratitude, the responses you've been seeking but not getting from others. Then seal the jar and focus on a pleasant and relaxing scene.

Finally, imagine yourself putting the jar aside somewhere—on a high shelf, perhaps, or in the trash can. Once you've put it aside, you'll have a chance to discover how mistaken you were in thinking that you needed approval and support from others in the first place. You'll find that you don't need others constantly telling you you're all right in order to feel that way. You'll learn that you don't need to feel disappointed, inadequate, and rejected every time your expectations don't materialize. Putting aside a symbolic container of self-destructive thoughts can trigger insight into your own real perceptions about yourself. If you practice this visualization technique every day or more often when you're feeling put upon by others—you'll soon find that your thoughts of rejection are just that: thoughts. As thoughts, they can be dismissed, modified, controlled.

12. I like the idea of doing something specific like that. Do you have other visualization exercises?

Yes, a technique like visualization can do more than get rid of negative feelings. It can also help you prepare yourself for positive ones—and for concrete successes. Remember what I said earlier about mentally picturing the events of each coming day in advance? Visualization techniques help psych you up for individual decisions and events. By preparing in advance, you'll greatly enhance your chances of success in actual encounters.

The English poet Robert Southey once told an amusing anecdote about a man who always put on special glasses when he was about to eat cherries, so that "they might look bigger and more tempting. In like manner," he said, "I make the most of my enjoyments, and though I do not cast my cares away, I pack them in as little compass as I can, and carry them as conveniently as I can for myself and never let them annoy others." The visualization exercises I've been describing are like Southey's friend's glasses. They can help make your pleasures more pleasurable, your achievements more likely. At the same time, using the "empty jar" technique can help you put your worries in "as little compass" as possible—and so make even more room for your successes.

The point is to learn to control your inner turmoil instead of having it control you. If you mentally allow yourself to experience specific feelings in relation to events and circumstances, you can move progressively through the stages of observation, analysis, and control. You can experience fear, self-doubt, competitiveness, acceptance, and joy without being taken over by any one of them.

When you can visualize the succession of events associated with a particular set of activities, especially those that appear frightening, you will be amazed at the abilities you are able to uncover and the extent of what you can accomplish.

Time and again in my work with Olympic athletes I have seen this demonstrated. By visualizing the perfect stroke, the perfect swing, or the perfect jump many times in the mind's eye, an athlete dramatically increases his chance of actually achieving it when he begins to perform. The more you can visualize the steps you will take in any activity, whether it is an athletic event, a job interview, or an exam, the better prepared you will be when the situation actually arises.

13. Can I use visualization to improve my concentration or increase my energy?

Visualization exercises can actually increase your skill in performing certain tasks, reduce your anxiety and tension (and thus your chances for error), and enhance your capacity to concentrate on critical issues. They are no less useful to you than to any Olympic athlete. I have seen the techniques work with young and old alike, many of whom were depressed. By repeatedly visualizing things that were only dreams when they first began to think about them, they managed to make them seem possible and thus were able to bring them about. By thinking through a project and focusing on the particular activities necessary to accomplish it, you endow yourself with energy and are able to accomplish far more than you ever imagined you could. We don't know precisely why this occurs, but it does.

14. Sometimes I think I don't really aim for success. How important is commitment to a task?

Very important. Successful people are committed people. Think about the dedication it takes to be a great athlete or scientist or dancer or anything

[123]

else. But most other people cop out about 85 percent of the time. You, too, may be afraid to commit yourself fully to what you want—because you think the inevitable failures won't look so bad if you give the task only half a try. Because you may not be comfortable going after what you want with all your energy, you approach your goals indirectly and spend time trying to get others to approve of you. You can change this, but first you must ask yourself how much time and energy you are willing to invest in what you're setting out do to. Are you focusing on the main objective or are you preoccupied with unresolved conflicts from the past? The process of growth is complex. You must be careful not to spend so much time justifying what you did in the past that you ignore new situations that can develop your talents and capacities.

15. *Are you saying that I'm responsible for my own success?*

Yes, indeed. Most people like to deny responsibility for what happens to them. They like to blame mates, bosses, parents. And they feel frustrated by many demands of convention, social pressure, and divided loyalties. But you've probably made little concrete effort to change or modify your own responses to those demands so as to make things better for yourself. Doing that, as I hope you're beginning to see, is an essential initial step toward self-control—and contentment.

I know it's difficult to accept the view that you are the one creating the stress in your life. But this is your life, and you are responsible for what you do, the circumstances you create, and what you get (or don't get) out of each day. You play a critical role—indeed, the most critical role—in the events that occur to you. Recognizing that is a start toward shaping them to your advantage.

Don't think I'm blaming you, or trying to make you feel guilty, for what has happened to you up to now. I know it's tough to face these truths without help, and as happened to me, perhaps no one has ever told you about helicopters. Understanding that things can be different, however, is the first step toward changing them. I hope the techniques I've outlined here will give you a push, and that you'll remind yourself every day of the central point I've been trying to make: It isn't them, it's you. *You can change your life.*